(y

ꙅꙍɒqꙅ

Creating Sensory Spaces celebrates spaces enlivened with sensual richness and provides you with the knowledge and tools necessary to create them. Drawing on numerous built case studies in ten countries and illustrated with over 85 full color images, the book presents a new framework for the design of sensory spaces including light, color, temperature, smell, sound and touch. Bridging across disciplines of architecture, engineering, phenomenology and perceptual psychology, this book informs the design of buildings and neighborhoods that reclaim the role of the body and all the senses in creating memorable experiences of place and belonging.

Barbara Erwine is an architectural design and research consultant and lecturer at the University of Washington, USA. Drawing on her background in science and architecture, her work, ranging from commercial buildings to sustainable urban master plans, integrates passive design strategies with architectural place-making. An advocate for sustainability, she helped develop one of the first US cohousing communities, where she now resides.

Creating Sensory Spaces

The Architecture of the Invisible

Barbara Erwine

NEW YORK AND LONDON

First published 2017
by Routledge
711 Third Avenue, New York, NY 10017

and by Routledge
2 Park Square, Milton Park, Abingdon, Oxon OX14 4RN

Routledge is an imprint of the Taylor & Francis Group, an informa business

© 2017 Taylor & Francis

The right of Barbara Erwine to be identified as author of this work has been
asserted by her in accordance with sections 77 and 78 of the Copyright, Designs
and Patents Act 1988.

All rights reserved. No part of this book may be reprinted or reproduced or utilized
in any form or by any electronic, mechanical, or other means, now known or
hereafter invented, including photocopying and recording, or in any information
storage or retrieval system, without permission in writing from the publishers.

Trademark notice: Product or corporate names may be trademarks or registered
trademarks, and are used only for identification and explanation without intent to
infringe.

Library of Congress Cataloging in Publication Data
Names: Erwine, Barbara, author.
Title: Creating sensory spaces : the architecture of the invisible / Barbara Erwine.
Description: New York : Routledge, 2017. | Includes bibliographical references and
index.
Identifiers: LCCN 2016020641| ISBN 9781138918764 (hardback : alk. paper)
 | ISBN 9781138918771 (pbk. : alk. paper) | ISBN 9781315688282 (ebook)
Subjects: LCSH: Senses and sensation in architecture. | Architecture--
Human factors.
Classification: LCC NA2543.S47 E79 2017 | DDC 720.1--dc23 LC record available at
https://lccn.loc.gov/2016020641

ISBN: 978-1-138-91876-4 (hbk)
ISBN: 978-1-138-91877-1 (pbk)
ISBN: 978-1-315-68828-2 (ebk)

Acquisition Editor: Wendy Fuller
Editorial Assistant: Grace Harrison
Production Editor: Alanna Donaldson

Typeset in Calvert
by Servis Filmsetting Ltd, Stockport, Cheshire

Cover image credit: Sea Organ and Greeting to the Sun: Women dance in
celebration of the sunset at Nikola Bašić's sound and light creation at the edge of
the Aegean Sea in Zadar, Croatia. Wave action generates a haunting melody and
LED lights powered by photovoltaics provide a coordinated light show (Architect:
Nikola Bašić, Marinaprojekt d.o.o.; photographer: Filip Brala).

Printed and bound in the United States of America by Sheridan

Contents

Acknowledgments

As I have worked to bring together the many related and yet disparate fields of sensory design presented here, I have been both humbled and amazed by the passionate voices and rigorous depth of work that has gone before. I am indebted to all of the visionary designers, scholars, researchers and educators who have inspired me with their wisdom and passion for places that are grounded in the body and reawaken us to the realm of the senses. Although they are too numerous to name here, the works and words of many of them appear in the pages that follow. I hope that I have done them justice. I am also grateful for the helpful discussions and encouragement I received from my wonderfully generous and learned colleagues in the Society of Building Science Educators to whom I first presented this work and who wholeheartedly responded with new ideas, resources and those dangerous words of "I think there is a book in there."

Many people reviewed the early drafts, providing technical feedback and massaging the words into a more graceful rhythm. For the generous gift of their time and talent, my heartfelt thanks goes out to Peter Berliner, Keith Simon and Barry Blesser, to my editors at Routledge, Wendy Fuller, Grace Harrison and Alanna Donaldson, and to Maggie Reid. I also want to thank the students of my Architecture 498 seminar class at the University of Washington for the helpful discussions we had on these topics and their explorations and observations of sensory spaces here in Seattle.

I have deep gratitude to all of the architects and photographers who have so generously contributed their photographs of buildings and sensescapes around the world. These images are vital to support the words in evoking the feeling of place. I especially want to thank Heli Ojamaa for her enthusiasm for this work and for the contribution of her images from her architectural travels through Scandinavia and Estonia.

And finally, my thanks goes out to my friends, family and cohousing community who have sustained me through this work—who encouraged me when the words did not flow, put up with me when I was overwhelmed and celebrated the finish of each chapter. My Friday writing group kept me focused, surrounding me with their company and encouragement in this lonely act of writing. My daughter Annie has sustained me with her bright energy and patience for my preoccupation in this past year. And special gratitude to Paul, my partner in life, who has massaged the tension out of my shoulders, poured me gin and tonics and steadily held forth his faith in me and the vision for this work when I seemed to have misplaced it somewhere beneath the heap of books and papers piled up on the floor of my writing room.

Image Credits

5.11 Architect: National Park Service and Denver Service Center; photo: Robb Williamson/NREL

5.12 This image has been reprinted with permission from the National Renewable Energy Laboratory. Paul Torcellini et al. (2004) *Zion National Park Visitor Center: Performance of a Low-Energy Building in a Hot Dry Climate*. NREL Report No. NREL/CP-550-36272 (accessed March 4, 2016).

5.13 Photo: Heli Ojamaa

6.1 Photo: author

6.2 Photo: Patrick Landy known as FSU Guy at en.wikipedia/CC BY

6.3 Architect/Source: Shea Trahan

6.4 Architect/Design: Sasaki, Dawson and DeMay; photo: author

6.5 Architect/Design: Sasaki, Dawson and DeMay; photo: author

6.6 Photo: author

6.7 Artist: Dan Corson; photo: author

7.1 Photo: author

7.2 Photo: author

7.3 Photo: author

7.4 Photo: Spedona/CC BY

7.5 Architecture: MODU; CFD analysis: ISOENV

7.6 Architect: Erik Gunnar Asplund; photo: Heli Ojamaa

8.1 Source: Valerie Mace; based on work by Malnar and Vodvarka

8.2 Source: Raymond Lucas

8.3 Photo: author

8.4 Photo: author

8.5 Source: author

8.6 Manufacturer: EGE Atelier

8.7 Architect: Doug Aitken; photo: Ye Rin Mok

8.8 Architect: Steven Holl Architects; photo: author

8.9 Architect: Steven Holl Architects; photo: author

Introduction

Paints, charcoals, fabrics and easels were the landscape of my childhood home. My mother was an artist and I spent much of my youth painting and writing poetry—exploring shapes and patterns, colors, textures and rhythms. I was drawn to the subtle, the hidden, the mysterious. But I was also fascinated by things logical and analytical. I loved the mental challenge of solving problems that had concrete answers. With this diverse background, my career could have gone many different directions, but I started my working life as a chemist. This was not because I had a passion for the binding of atoms into molecules but because when I was in high school, any young woman who demonstrated a proclivity for the "hard sciences" was funneled toward them, a representative of her gender in a male-dominated field. After 13 years as an analytical chemist, I recognized that although chemistry engaged my analytical mind, it did not draw my artistic heart. So I began searching for a lifework that would celebrate both the amorphic creativity of my right brain and the analytic problem-solving of my left. I entered a graduate program in architecture with the goal of applying both of these to my growing interest in sustainability.

There, in the mid 1980s, I was surprised to encounter a schism that I have since seen play out in universities and design teams around the United States. In shorthand, it was called "Architecture, with a capital A" versus engineering (or design versus building science). In longhand, it spanned much more nuanced territory. With a foot planted firmly on each side of this divide, I found myself straddling these two perspectives and frequently playing the role of translator between them. This split had ramifications for the design of sensory space. In our vision-centered culture, the design side had become increasingly (although often unfairly) judged predominantly by the visual aspects of the work. The engineers on the other side attended to most of the other sensory realms (temperature, light, acoustics and air quality), often with an analytical focus on measureable indices of safety and comfort. Although each side usually maintained a healthy respect for the other, they tended to do so at a distance.

The recent emphasis on an integrated design process has significantly narrowed this gap between disciplines. This integration is not just about working together, but is also about developing language and frameworks to think differently about the problems and opportunities we encounter. In his chapter in *Biophilic Design*, Edward O. Wilson notes how the most important work of our times lies at the intersection of different mindsets that approach each other over a critical question of interest.[1] Surely the design and engineering of the sensory realms are at this intersection. Working together toward the goal of beautiful and sustainable places that speak to our hearts, these two perspectives sculpt the same space with different but complementary languages, tools and professional degrees. In the process of bridging this gap, I have come to be an observant student of the sensory realms as "shaped entities" in the environment—rooms and alcoves of light and warmth, sound, texture and smell. These sensory nodes create independent volumes of sensory space that must be designed together with the geometry of walls, openings and physical enclosures as we shape the built environment.

As this book explores how these shaped sensory spaces work together with the geometry of form, we will encounter another gap—that which exists between the constructed forms (whether material or sensory) and the sense of place that arises from them. This movement between the creation and the experience is the leap that is required in all art—poetry, music, theater, painting and architecture. It is the leap that happens when words in a sequence or colored strokes on a canvas suddenly transform into a pang in the heart. We experience this gap when moving from the words of a poem to the depth of the poem's meaning. Take, for example, the following haiku by Bashō:

"Poverty's child—
he starts to grind the rice,
and gazes at the moon."[2]

Simple words, describing a simple scene: a poor child grinding rice looks at the moon. But the words also transcend the scene to evoke deep feelings that may at first seem unrelated to the words themselves. We may be caught by a sharp poignancy, an appreciation of humanity and beauty. We may be struck by the understanding that even a poor child alone at night with a task to do can find beauty in the moon. That perhaps in the end, we are all poor children grinding rice, gazing at the moon, becoming lost in its beauty, its promise, its hope, its transcendence. That there is both this world with its tangible rice and poverty and there is also something else. These meanings arise from the words of the poem and yet we can't find them within any particular word or any single line of the poem. At each reading, they arise from the interaction between the entirety of the poem and the reader him/herself. To experience this depth, we can't merely read the poem—we have to inhabit it.

A similar leap happens between the design of space and the creation of place. Our great buildings have walls and ceilings, enclosures and openings; they have light and darkness; they have areas of warmth, sounds that reverberate at specific frequencies and odors that linger. But just as the words of a poem do not create the longing, the hope, the melancholy (it was there within us all along), so the geometry and sensory attributes of a design do not alone create the sense of place; they only encourage us to linger so that sense can emerge. No one of them holds the sense of place that is evoked; not even the overlap of all of them holds that sense of place. And yet, neither does it exist independently of them. This leap is the transformation of stone, warmth and flickering light to hearth and home.

With problems that are this complex, where neither side of the divide seems to have the perfect toolset, I used to think that a completely new toolset was needed. And perhaps that is the case. But more often these days, I think that what is important is that we do not get too invested in the tools that we use, that we hold them more lightly in our hands knowing that they are imperfect but that they are all that we have. Whether our tool is a scientific measure or a napkin sketch of the essence of place, at best it helps us to hold a vision and communicate it as we craft the built environment and make it our home.

As we explore the design of sensory space in this book, we will consider both sides of this divide, and at some point, we will make the leap. It will not always be graceful. There will be a disconnection as we jump from left brain to right, from mind to heart. And just as we must inhabit the poem to feel its meaning, we can't just stand back and look at a built place; we have to inhabit it and feel it around us. Only then may we come to love our creations.

The problems we face as we encounter the limits of sustainability on our finite planet require both our analytical intellect and our heart or we will not survive, let alone thrive. The pages that follow and the insightful works that they reference pursue a sensory design approach that moves us from sustainability to thriving, from comfort to delight. When it falls short, as surely any ambitious work must, I urge the reader to pick up the work we have started here and move it forward into our collective future.

Notes

1   Edward O. Wilson, "The nature of human nature," chapter 2 in *Biophilic Design*, ed. Stephen R. Kellert, Judith H. Heerwagen, and Martin L. Mador (New Jersey: John Wiley & Sons, 2008), 21.

2   Matsuo Bashō as noted in Philip J. Adler and Randall L. Pouwels, *World Civilizations: Volume II: Since 1500* (Boston: Wadsworth Cengage Learning, 2012), 385.

The World is Flat

Chapter 1

"It is absurdly easy to build, and appallingly easy to build badly. Comfort is confused with the absence of sensation."[1]

Bloomer and Moore

A salmon flies through the air in a slippery glide toward the outstretched arms of a fishmonger behind a mountain of ice and splayed flesh. One cold, lifeless fish eye catches mine before it lands with a slap and a spray of ice. It's a show for the tourists as they shout and snap selfies with their iPhones. Yet this exuberant spectacle still has a certain allure for me after a quarter-century of Seattle living. The chill of the ice, the acrid tinge of brine and day-old fish, the cacophony of laughter and haggling; this is the heart of Seattle's beloved market, the oldest continually operating farmers' market in the United States (Figure 1.1). But the market is also the showy color of flowers in early spring, the halo of Christmas carols in December, the musky patchouli oils, the warmth of a deep fryer turning out fresh donuts, the taste of clam chowder, the aroma of baked bread, the harmony of two buskers strumming guitar and mandolin, the stink of piss in dark corners and the antiseptic pine-scented cleanser floating above it, the tinge of curry, the jostle of crowds spilling out into the warmth of sunlight or the chilly drizzle of a light rain. Carry it in your heart or avoid it like the plague, this is Seattle's Pike Place Market, as it has been for the past 100 years, in all its sensuous, tawdry glory, in all its seasons. Attracting tourists and locals alike, it

Figure 1.1 Pike Place Market, alive with smells, sounds, sights and textures, is a popular tourist attraction and a beloved Seattle tradition.

The World is Flat

is just this delight of the senses that makes the market an event in itself, elevating this old warehouse space into a memorable *place*.

Perhaps part of the attraction rests in just how rare this delight of the senses is in our modern world. The historically lush and sensuous built environments we evolved in have paled to a relatively bland, homogeneous palette. With ever-increasing technological accuracy, the places we now design and build are controlled to narrowly acceptable ranges of temperature, light, smell, sound, texture and color. We inhabit engineered environments controlled to be efficient and agreeable to the "average" person. In our quest for comfort, we often neglect delight. We work in standardized offices with a uniform temperature of 68°F (20°C), a light level of 50 footcandles (538 lux), sound masking of 47 decibels and background trace odors at the level of parts per million (Figure 1.2).

But as Pike Place Market demonstrates, this was not always the case. We come from a rich history of buildings,

neighborhoods, parks and cities with an elaborate tapestry of sensory delights. They present a lush sensory landscape, a "sensescape" of peaks and valleys of color, texture, sound, smell and light that speak to us of our place in the world. Just

Figure 1.2 Uniform light levels in modern buildings were aimed at ensuring comfortable working light for everyone, but when taken to an extreme, this practice results in uninteresting lighting with no sense of place.

mentioning a sensory aspect can evoke the whole memory of a place—the smell of freshly baked bread as you pass a Parisian *boulangerie*, the shaft of light that fingers its way along the walls of the Pantheon, the feel of cobblestone in the streets of Georgetown, the reverberant overtones of a Gregorian chant in the chapel at Sant'Anselmo. This colorful heritage of smells, sounds, lights and textures immerses us in the world around us.

THE JOURNEY TO SENSORY DEPRIVATION

A number of seemingly unrelated causes interacted to transport us from this rich sensory heritage to the state of sensory homogeneity that is becoming synonymous with our modern world. The first of these is the growing dominance of vision in the hierarchy of the senses. Malnar and Vodvarka credit this "hegemony of the eye" to the Renaissance discovery of the two-point perspective and the visual representations of buildings in plan, section and elevation.[2] Before that time, the human species was more focused on smells and sounds.[3] However, we can find reverence for sight in the panoply of senses in Western culture at least as far back as Aristotle, who accorded sight as the most highly developed of the human senses.[4] It is the sense of clear thinking, the sense of the mind. It is clean and precise. But it also is distancing, placing the observer outside the scene. The other senses provide interactive, immersive experiences. You have to be close to something to smell or touch it, but vision can happen at a safe, antiseptic distance.

The modernist idiom carried forward and reinforced the dominance of visual impact. We have become an "ocular-centric" profession, prioritizing visual impact over engagement of the other senses and dependent on our eyes alone to evaluate "good" design. Juhani Pallasmaa laments "this bias towards vision, and the suppression of other senses, in the way architecture is conceived, taught and critiqued, and … the disappearance of sensory and sensual qualities from the arts and architecture."[5] This bias is reinforced by most architectural publications and design competitions which present images of projects, usually without people in them, and focus on the space from a single-point perspective. These articles rarely recount what it actually feels like to be in the space. This creates a gap between the mental construct of design and the physical, immersive world that is inhabited. Sensitive architects and designers bemoan this preoccupation with the visual when they have invested so much more depth in their projects. Pallasmaa poignantly reminds us of this narcissistic and nihilistic eye as he notes that "modernist design at large has housed the intellect and the eye, but it has left the body and the other senses, as well as our memories, imaginations and dreams, homeless."[6]

A second influence that helped lead the way toward the uniformity of sensory design was an altruistic one—the humanitarian desire to provide a base level of comfort for everyone. Arising from the Industrial Revolution when human environments changed dramatically and people were subjected to harsh work and home conditions, it was a noble action to guarantee minimum standards of lighting, sound, air pollution, etc. These were essential moves to care for the common man in a world focused on production. But this narrow focus sometimes left the design world satisfied with attaining just this minimum.

The precise engineering approach of the twentieth century was based on research studies that evaluated an average population's basic needs for survival and preferences for comfort and productivity. It identified basic comfort thresholds and set these as minimum standards for building performance. These standards represent the point where no more than 20 percent of the population will complain about the environment. The standards don't address whether any one of that population will be delighted by it, will find joy or inspiration or will be moved to a deep connection to place.

As designers of the physical realm, architects and engineers were empowered to implement these standards in the mid-twentieth century by advancements that gave them precise control over a building's environment and by what appeared to be unlimited energy resources to maintain this narrow band of sensory conditions. The result was a cultural norm with closely controlled ranges of temperature, light, smell and sound. Experiments were conducted; comfort charts were drawn; light levels were targeted; and elaborate electrical/mechanical systems were engineered to maintain the identified "comfort conditions" over every square foot of building space through every occupied hour of the day.

Historically, mankind has benefited greatly from the elimination of environmental extremes that these systems guaranteed. Incorporated into generally accepted standards like ISO, ASHRAE, ANSI, etc., these environmental precautions saved workers from the poor air quality and dimly lit interior spaces of earlier times. However, within Vitruvius' trilogy of firmness, commodity and delight, stopping at standards leaves design stalled at the level of commodity with nothing to say about delight. If we stop the design process with the achievement of these standards, we regulate ourselves into a corner of sensory mediocrity. The replication of this approach results in spaces that are everywhere the same and nowhere special—environments that are acceptable but not inspiring, comfortable but not comforting, predictable but not memorable. The systems to maintain this consistency overdraw the Earth's resources and, in exchange, return environments with no sense of place, time or cultural identity.

Yet, this doesn't have to be. The standards are just minimum acceptable values; they are not the end goal of good design. So as we honor these standards for the benefits they provide, we must also reclaim the diversity and richness of a multisensory world, not just as engineered habitat for survival but as integrated, connected, fully celebrated place.

The structure of the design profession itself provides a third impetus toward the flattening of our sensory world. Architects and designers are trained to conceive of design with acute sensitivity to the shape of planes coming together in space and the three-dimensional voids they create between them. But their education does not give the same attention to the shape of *sensory* spaces. The field of sensory design falls into the cracks between several traditional disciplines and is frequently overlooked. In particular, the built environment professions have evolved toward a separation between the architects or urban planners who design the space and the engineering professionals who, in large part, create their sensory phenomena. As noted above, the move toward standards-based sensory design has oriented engineers toward a scientific/analytical process focused on uniformity and not on experiential delight. Bloomer and Moore acknowledge this predisposition in *Body, Memory, and Architecture*, pointing out that

> "The basic purpose of developing schools of engineering was to establish the precise rules governing the objective performance of physical operations, not to consider the emotional experience of human beings. (Unfortunately, by these standards, a specific work of architecture from the past could be declared generally

inferior because of its awkward and less efficient technical resolution even if it gave to its inhabitants a superior feeling of joy and satisfaction.)"[7]

These resulting silos of responsibility—the designer and the engineer—are often seen as representing the right brain/left brain, heart/mind, emotion/logic dualism in our contemporary approach to problems. This duality sometimes plays out in stereotypes of the professions. Architects may characterize engineers as rigid and non-creative; engineers may portray architects/designers as emotional, unrealistic and impractical.

To accomplish the paradigm shift required to implement full sensory design, the current silos of design and engineering must evolve to form a new integrated/collaborative relationship. As the rewards of this new paradigm unfold, designers (architects, urban planners, interior designers, landscape architects, etc.) will move to embrace the traditional engineering realms of environmental controls and engineers will claim their due place in the design arena. This holistic design approach must respect the needs for comfort without losing sight of the opportunities for wonderfully rich and varied sensory experiences. In order for this to happen, we must also draw on knowledge from psychology, physiology, sociology and anthropology to provide vital information on how people actually perceive space and develop preferences (individually and culturally). Thus the design of the sensory realm falls at the intersection of multiple responsibilities and will only thrive when a truly integrated and body-centered approach emerges.

The final culprit in the attenuation of sensory environments is the modern concept of generic design and the speculative development market that promoted it. In this paradigm, buildings and entire neighborhoods are designed and built for a generic client—the so-called "average consumer." In the mid-twentieth century, architectural design embraced the concept of space as a disembodied commodity that could be designed for any place on Earth to serve a variety of changing functions. Driven by the efficiency of flexibility and the egalitarian platform of uniformity, this approach to design fosters the creation of a blank slate to be filled in by the eventual occupant. But before the occupant arrives, most of the systems that affect sensory experience are already installed as part of the blank slate background. So the experience of the occupant who is *in* the space is often sacrificed to the house that is designed for drive-by street appeal or the corporate headquarters that uses its building's façade to advertise and reinforce its brand and business proposition. As Pallasmaa notes, "instead of an existentially grounded plastic and spatial experience, architecture has adopted the psychological strategy of advertising and instant persuasion; buildings have turned into image products detached from existential depth and sincerity."[8]

At the urban scale, this attenuation of the sensescape may act to obscure or even obliterate the cultural identity of an entire neighborhood. The traditional activities of an area's occupants include associated sensory qualities that imbue that place with a familiar and recognizable sensory culture. Too often, urban rehabilitation projects attempting to recreate a preexisting cultural identity mimic the visual symbols of culture while obliterating other more "problematic" sensory cues (smells, sounds, textures, etc.) that are essential to the cultural experience. Pardy calls this a depoliticizing of space which makes these rehabilitated neighborhoods "sites of *display* rather than sites of *dwelling* where authentic engagement with diversity is avoided and a palatable non-confronting version of multiculturalism is promoted."[9]

RECLAIMING PLACE

As Western culture has become a culture of the eye, the separation this creates between observer and that which is observed has contributed to the culture of the "I." As we stand back to see, we also remove ourselves from the world, and this taints our perspective of our place in it. We see ourselves as users or stewards, not as fully immersed and active participants. This action disembodies us—from our own bodies and from the body of this living, changing planet. It emphasizes the distance of the cool, rational mind, not the messy interaction of the body immersed in place.

Full sensory space, on the other hand, is an embodied place, a place of dwelling. Benedikt examines the difference between vision-centric "exteriorist design," which places us as observers outside the space, and sensory-rich "interiorism," which places us within an enveloping spatial experience (see Figures 1.3 and 1.4). Acknowledging that contemporary architecture, and the field of design in general, usually takes the exteriorist perspective, he notes that "the lack of a way to describe and map sensory experience and to make it a part of design plagues the field to this day, notwithstanding the comparative ease with which 'perspectives' can be generated by CAD software."[10]

Responding to the need for paradigm change that recognizes the significance of both interiorist and exteriorist perspectives, this book explores each of the sensory realms one by one in the following chapters and probes how each can be shaped to create fully immersive sensory experiences. This exploration is written from the perspective of a fully sighted person in an ocular-centric culture. Although it briefly touches on the experiences of

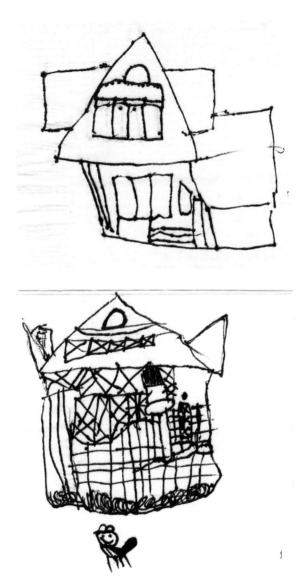

Figures 1.3 and 1.4 When asked to draw a napkin sketch of a house, two six-year-old twins, Liam and Lillia, each came from a different perspective. Liam's drawing (top) stands back from the house to give us a cleanly organized exteriorist view, while Lillia's drawing (bottom) immerses us in the rich and complex relationships of an interiorist experience.

people who are visually impaired and thus more dependent on other sensory inputs, it does this more to explore the wide range of abilities available to those who have worked to expand their sensory sensitivity. The observations about sensory interactions might be different for partially sighted or non-sighted people, or for cultures that have honed other senses to take a more balanced role in the perceptual field.

Our senses constitute the whole of our interaction with the physical world, yet many of them only enter the design discussion when they pose a problem like an offensive odor coming from an adjacent factory or the irritating sound of freeway traffic disrupting a quiet repose. The work before us is to expand this discussion and its place within the design process. The work will take some effort, but it will be worth it. As Bachelard reminds us, "if we multiplied images, taking them in the domains of lights and sounds, of heat and cold, we should prepare a slower ontology, but doubtless one that is more certain than the ontology that reposes upon geometrical images."[11] As we experience and fully embody this sensory world, we will hone our awareness of sensory experiences and develop a language to express them. Moving away from sensory realms flattened by uniformity and standardization, we will learn to shape spaces of sound, smell, texture, color, light and temperature and to celebrate this architecture of the invisible.

Notes

1 Kent C. Bloomer and Charles W. Moore, *Body, Memory, and Architecture* (New Haven: Yale University Press, 1977), 105.
2 Joy Monice Malnar and Frank Vodvarka, *Sensory Design* (Minneapolis: University of Minnesota Press, 2004), 11.
3 Juhani Pallasmaa, *The Eyes of the Skin: Architecture and the Senses* (West Sussex: John Wiley & Sons, 2005), 25.
4 Malnar and Vodvarka, *Sensory Design*, 11.
5 Pallasmaa, *The Eyes of the Skin*, 10.
6 Ibid., 19.
7 Bloomer and Moore, *Memory, and Architecture*, 21.
8 Pallasmaa, *The Eyes of the Skin*, 30.

The World is Flat

9   Pardy cited in Kelum Palipane, "Towards a sensory production of urban space: developing a conceptual framework of inquiry based on socio-sensory perception" (Paper presented at the International RC21 Conference, *The struggle to Belong: Dealing with Diversity in 21st Century Urban Settings*, Amsterdam, July 7–9, 2011), 3.
10 Michael Benedikt, "Environmental Stoicism and Place Machismo," *Harvard Design Magazine* 16, Winter/Spring (2002), 4.
11 Gaston Bachelard, *The Poetics of Space* (Boston: Beacon Press, 1969), 215.

Celebration of the Senses

Chapter 2

"The voices of the past do not sound the same
in the big room as in the little bed chamber,
and calls on the stairs have yet another sound.
Among the most difficult memories, well beyond
any geometry that can be drawn, we must
recapture the quality of the light; then come the
sweet smells that linger in the empty rooms,
setting an aerial seal on each room in the house
of memory."[1]

Gaston Bachelard

Clinging to the base of a forested hill, Alki Beach looks across Puget Sound toward stunning views of the Olympic Mountains. One of the few white sand beaches in Seattle, Alki offers a soft contrast to adjacent rocky shorelines. On summer nights, it is a gathering spot for a multigenerational, multiethnic mix of Seattle's youth, families and elders. Along the beach, people gather early in the day to claim one of the most coveted party venues in the city. As night closes in, the parties are visible as a series of glowing campfires dotting the beach with an inky darkness filling the space between them. Approach one and you have entered a private realm, enclosed by neither walls nor doors but still a clear definition of place, carved out of the brisk night air. Light, heat and sound alone mark the threshold of these intimate gatherings. Step into the fire's sphere of warmth and you have entered the heart of the party; step four feet back and you're "out in the cold" so to speak, outside the action and alone.

The experience of a campfire (Figure 2.1) expands our understanding of the ways in which we create spaces in the world. As we move around throughout a day, we consciously step across recognizable boundaries of architectural tectonic spaces. We are so aware of them that their constructed elements represent some of the early words in a child's vocabulary. We name the volumes they create as house, room, alcove, courtyard, plaza, etc. We name their bounding elements, both side to side (walls) and top to bottom (ceilings/floors). We even name their connecting pieces—door, window, threshold, hallway. We are less adept at noticing and naming the location, volumes and transitions of sensory spaces. Yet sensory experiences occupy volumes of space and have beginnings and endings, entries and borders, just as the geometry of architectural space does. And as designers,

Figure 2.1 exterior (above) and interior (below) This delightful warming hut in a school play yard takes its shape from the thermal space that it encloses (HAUGEN/ZOHAR Arkitekter, Trondheim, 2009).

Celebration of the Senses

we can become just as adept at shaping these invisible spaces. We can create cathedrals of smell, caves of sound, alcoves of warmth, thresholds of texture, cones of light. This invisible architecture not only enriches the tectonic space it overlaps but can effectively subdivide it into separate interior spaces or extend it beyond its prescribed walls.

A SENSE OF THE WORLD

As children, we learn that the human body has five senses: sight, hearing, touch, taste and smell. This framework dates back at least as far as Aristotle's *De Anima*, which devotes a chapter to each sense. But today our understanding of biological systems is much more complex. Many neurologists now identify 9 or more senses, and some claim there are over 20. Sometimes they are identified by the sensory organ used for detection; sometimes they are differentiated by the type of detector within the sense organ; and at other times, they are divided up by the type of information conveyed and where it is processed in the body. In an attempt to condense the categories, Christian Jarrett suggests in his book *Great Myths of the Brain* that

> "if we restrict our definition of a discrete sense to the physical categories of incoming information, we can simplify the human senses down to just three—mechanical (which takes in touch and hearing), chemical (including taste, smell and internal senses) and light."[2]

For all of these categorization systems, the underlying question is—what exactly do we count as a sense? The sense of touch, for example, is usually considered part of our somatosensory system, which includes the common experiences of texture, pressure, pain and temperature. But less commonly recognized aspects of this sensory system are the signals that allow us to know where our body parts are without looking at them (proprioception), the ability to know the position of our bodies relative to gravity, and information about the state of our inner body (hunger, thirst and the need to urinate or sneeze, etc.). Do we count each of these as senses, or is it appropriate to lump them together into a single sense of touch? Each of the original five sensory realms has a similar level of complexity, and there is no clear consensus on the divisions among them.

In fact, the mere act of dividing up our sensory interactions with the world into discrete detection mechanisms is fraught with error. For our sensory systems are not really separate, independently operating input machines that conduct a one-way transmission of information from the world to our brain. More accurately, human perception, as we now understand it, is an intricate, integrated and overlapping interaction between the body and the world around it. Gibson conceived of the senses as aggressive seeking mechanisms, not merely passive sensation receivers.[3] In explaining Merleau-Ponty's phenomenological understanding, Hass explores this two-way interaction further, noting that our sensory systems are communication channels or openings to the world and referring to perception as a "field of contact with otherness."[4] He notes that

> "Perception is not 'inside me' like a beetle in a box, but rather emerges between my organizing, sensing body and the things of the world … an interacting field that emerges at the nexus of its participants and which we call experience."[5]

So we're not outside of our perceptions, watching them like a movie on a screen, but rather we participate with them in an intimate and interactive two-way relationship with the world.

Stretching our understanding of the senses even further, in his chapter in *Mind in Architecture*, Juhani Pallasmaa suggests the idea of an "atmospheric sense" as the sixth

Celebration of the Senses

sense. He postulates that as humans, we first have a sense of place or sense of "atmosphere" of place that is active before we attune to individual sensory perceptions.[6] This addresses the existence of a "meaningful whole" that is perceived initially as an entirety rather than being the mere summation of individual sensory experiences. This also aligns with Mark Johnson's chapter in the same book, which addresses one of Dewey's ideas, noting that

"in addition to specific sensory qualities, every situation we encounter is unified and marked off by what he called its 'pervasive unifying quality.' … Dewey's argument is that only within such a unified situation do we then experience individual objects, persons, and events, with their particular qualities and affordances. … Consequently, any encounter with an architectural structure begins with the overall sense of place (of being in a particular world), followed almost immediately by a growing grasp of the numerous meanings afforded by its various parts, light patterns, structural relations, contrasts, flow, rhythms, and other significant elements of meaning within the work."[7]

The progression of these ideas moves us further and further from a simplistic view of five basic senses, each with its own dedicated sense organ that reports objective, unbiased data about a concrete world, and brings us closer to understanding the wonderfully subjective nature of our perceptual world. Add to this the fact that we each bring our personal and cultural filters to the sensory experience—our upbringing, past experiences, physiology, preferences, dislikes and expectations—and we begin to understand the different sensory worlds we inhabit. For example, of four people sitting in a symphony audience, one may be enveloped in the symphonic sound, one may be consumed by irritation at the person to the right of them who is crunching on a throat lozenge, one may be so chilly that the music is a backdrop to the discomfort of cold and one may be lost in thought about an upcoming work crisis and relatively oblivious to the sensory inputs. Although they are all in the same sensory field, each of these people has a dramatically different sensory experience.

The most extensive research into these sensory differences and filters has been done with people who lack sight, the dominant sensory mode in Western culture. Blind and visually impaired people frequently have heightened abilities in their other senses to provide information for navigating the world. The experiences of non-sighted people show us how we can hear the presence of walls and grade changes or smell our way through a building to its kitchen. These heightened abilities are available to all of us and yet are not honed by necessity and thus lie dormant. So, clearly, not all sensory inputs make it to our conscious perception.

Thus, as we can see, our relationship with the sensescape becomes more and more nuanced as scholars of the field continue their investigations and debate. However, the design and construction of the built environment generally deals with infrastructure systems and specialties whose impact falls roughly into the original five categories of touch, taste, hearing, sight and smell. With the exception of taste, there are many clear examples of how architects, engineers, interior designers, urban planners and landscape architects manipulate one or more of their design decisions to specifically impact these sensory categories. Whether it is the engineer sizing and locating duct work for the heating, ventilation and air conditioning (HVAC) system, the architect designing a clerestory window, the interior designer choosing a color palette, or the landscape architect specifying an aromatic herb to line a pathway, each of these actions directly impacts the sensescape and can be loosely categorized within the simplistic framework of five basic senses.

So this book takes two approaches at opposite ends of the conceptual framework. The first is to explore the built environment under relatively condensed categories that reflect the infrastructure and specialties common to the building industry. This includes light space (vision), somatic space (touch, texture and movement), thermal space (part of the somatic senses, but addressed separately here because of its architectural infrastructure and associations in the built environment), acoustic space (hearing), olfactory space (smell) and private/cultural space (part of the sixth sense identified by Pallasmaa). We'll explore each sensory area's ability to shape our experience of the built environment and anticipate the impact of overlaps with other sensory modes. The second approach is to explore multisensory places as a whole and encourage the reader to go out and experience sensory spaces at firsthand. As we have noted, sensory experiences must be felt in the body—first, as a whole person interacting with a particular place and its pervasive unifying quality and, only after that, as a place with particular sensory attributes that contribute toward or detract from the overall ambiance. These sensory exercises will add the depth of experiential participation to the narrative descriptions in the book.

ARCHITECTURE OF THE INVISIBLE

This book represents an important shift of perception through its understanding of the sensescape as volumetric, shaped sensory spaces that can be inhabited—spaces of warmth, color, light, sound, smell and texture, and the personal and cultural spaces brought to life through habitual use patterns. We will come to see how these spaces exist independently of the tectonic constructions of walls, floors, ceilings, etc. that are the traditional purview of the architect. And like their tectonic counterparts, each of these sensory spaces has identifiable characteristics of location, shape, boundaries (rigid or porous), intensity, duration, etc., that can be designed and perceived. This new perspective lets us comprehend the experience of entering and leaving these sensory spaces. It lets us examine whether they are congruent with each other or dissonant, whether they build to intensify a cohesive experience or diverge to create an illusion (or just a bad design).

For example, I can remember the musky smell as I walked down the stairway into my grandmother's basement as a child. I don't remember the shape of the room at the bottom, but I can vividly recall the aroma of rotting apples mingling with the smell of damp earthen floor and the jumbled texture of old woven baskets, bottles and lawn ornaments. The mystery of the objects and odors contained in the cellar kept my concentration and I was oblivious to the shape of its walls. The primary experience that held it together as a space was the smell that permeated it, sometimes intensifying toward a basket of rotting apples and bleeding off to just a perceptible whiff at the top of the stairs. The olfactory space was not defined by the rectilinear walls, floor and ceiling, but consisted of a gradient field of sensation that created a series of sensory nodes—subspaces within the larger room that clustered around the aromatic fruit and objects in the space. At harvest time, the odors might be so intense that they reached past the cellar doorway to expand this olfactory space beyond its tectonic container.

Like tectonics, the boundaries of sensory space can be rigid or fluid, permanent or ephemeral, solid or porous. And while tectonic space leans toward the former in each of these pairings, sensory space leans toward the latter, thus bringing with it more magical qualities. Perhaps this is why the design profession has been slower to develop a vocabulary acknowledging its physical existence. But whether sensory spaces are ephemeral or long-lasting, they create inhabitable places in the world just as a set of four walls does. And often they linger in our memories longer than the walls.

At an urban scale, sensory design explores both the shape and rhythm of these sensory spaces across entire neighborhoods or cities. It notes whether the streetscape is experienced as a series of human-scale nodes alive with sounds, smells and tactile enticements from sidewalk vendors and musicians or as a monotonous tunnel droning with vehicular traffic and exhaust.

As we delve into this realm of the senses, we are indebted to many earlier voices that have provided wake-up calls to the rich sensescape that is our heritage. Christian Norberg-Schulz, for example, reminds us that in Prague, "the illumination is not continuous and even; strongly lit and dark zones alternate, and make us remember the times when a street lamp created a place."[8] Lisa Heschong's *Thermal Delight in Architecture* recalls the vitality of varied temperatures that draws people to cozy fireplaces in winter, cool courtyards in summer—spaces that invoke memories and a sense of place.[9] Juhani Pallasmaa admires the capacity of the human ear to carve a volume into the void of darkness.[10] And the writings of Victoria Henshaw invite us to take a walk through the urban "smellscape."[11] We will draw on the wisdom of these and other pioneers of sensory design as we explore this architecture of the invisible.

A WORLD OF DIFFERENCES

One of the first things that we notice in this exploration is that we experience everything in relation to a larger context. If the whole world is blue, then color becomes meaningless. Everywhere we look, smell, hear or feel, we perceive these experiences against a contrasting field. We see the red peony against the greenery surrounding it; we feel the warmth of a fire in contrast to the cold away from it. For something to be noticed, it must emerge from the background.

These sensory qualities are experienced as a continuum of possibilities with contrasts at the extremes. The contrast may be light/dark, rough/smooth, hot/cold, sloped/flat, redolent (scented)/odorless, etc. We sculpt sensory space using both sides of the sensory continuum of contrast. A bright cone of light around a dining table creates a lively gathering place for a group, while a dark corner may provide a secluded refuge for an amorous couple. Flat expanses are directionless and safe, but don't engage our muscles in the same way as sloping ramps. We exaggerate experiences by juxtaposing them with their contrasting opposites. Cold feels colder when you emerge from a warm building; silence seems more precious when it follows a loud outburst. Bachelard recognizes this in pointing out that "behind dark curtains, snow seems to be whiter. Indeed, everything comes alive when contradictions accumulate."[12] And Lisa Heschong acknowledges this as she transports us to the lush refuge of the Islamic garden (Figure 2.2).

"Perhaps the desire for contrast is a reason why the gardens of Islam had to be contained by high walls. The garden, with its flowers, shade trees, and fountains provided a cool refuge from the desert heat. The bright sun and hot desert air could not be completely excluded, but the walls sharply defined the limits of the garden and concentrated the sense of its lush coolness. Certainly, the high walls were a way to ensure privacy, so important for the Muslim. But the walls' highly visible presence also

Figure 2.2 The shaded entryway to a walled garden at the Alcázar in Sevilla frames a view of the lush coolness that awaits within.

served to emphasize the difference between the cool garden within and the hot desert without."[13]

Imperfections can represent interesting occurrences of contrast. For example, if we encounter a smooth surface with a small imperfection in it, we run our hand along it and return to the imperfection, worrying it with our fingertips. Does this imperfection lessen or heighten our experience of the smoothness of the surface? Or the tinge of rotting seaweed at the seashore—does it lessen or heighten the contrasting freshness of the sea breeze?

At what level of imperfection does the smooth surface become rough or the sea breeze become foul?

Among these contrasts, we develop both personal and cultural preferences based on pleasantness/ unpleasantness or affinity/aversion. The phenomenon of attraction or aversion depends on both the characteristics of the sensory phenomena and the internal conditions of the perceiver. A person who is very cold may perceive a room at 56°F (13°C) to be warm, while an overheated person will perceive it to be cold. This dependence of perception on interior conditions is known as alliesthesia.[14] At the extreme of unpleasantness (negative alliesthesia) for some sensations, we may experience pain or even death; for example, if temperatures drop too low. In addition to the physiologic preferences for sensory contrasts and combinations, many sensory realms carry with them strong emotional reactions. Frequently, these feelings of liking or disliking are associated with positive or negative memories. For example, a musky smell may conjure up pleasant memories of the ritual of incense in a Catholic church or it may trigger a fearful reaction to an unknown or decaying/rotting substance. The smell may be the same, but two different reactions emerge depending on the observer's personal history and culture. A corollary in somatic space is the experience of exposed heights, which thrill one person but trigger a huge fear reaction in the other. So as we explore each of the senses, we will also touch on these personal and cultural biases, noting how they attract or repel or otherwise direct behavior for the populations that inhabit spaces.

Commercial enterprises have taken note of this power of sensory space to attract people and encourage behaviors and have been quick to exploit it for marketing purposes. With the advent of air conditioning in the early 1900s, movie houses drew customers in by spilling cool air out onto the sidewalk to entice passersby with the promise of comfort on hot summer days. Today, in a similar fashion, the local Mrs. Fields store pumps the odor of freshly baked cookies out into the mall. Examples abound for the sensory marketing of everything, from patented scents that encourage consumers to pay $10 more for a pair of Nike running shoes to focused lighting that directs our gaze to the blouse with the highest profit margin in the store. According to one study: "Retailers should seriously consider ambient scent in their marketing toolbox. It is probably among one of the least expensive techniques to enhance shoppers perceptions. Product-related or congruent scent may be effective to increase the sales of a particular product."[15] The power of sensory cues has clearly grabbed the attention of commercial product marketers. But as we have seen, the building and urban design professions have, if anything, moved in the opposite direction, often leveling out the sensescape to a uniform flatness. It is time to consciously take up these powerful design tools of the senses to help shape an atmosphere of place.

THE SHAPE OF SENSORY PLACE

One challenge in designing the sensescape is the need to develop an understanding of shaped sensory spaces that inherently are not apparent to the human eye. We understand the visual shapes created by walls and openings, but the volume of sound in a church apse is more difficult to comprehend. We may get some visual cues to its existence but, ultimately, must enter it to feel its full presence and extent. Architect and visionary Sean Lally recognizes the physicality of these sensory spaces as variations in energy fields across space, since the primary sensory signals—the "inputs" (heat, sound, light, chemical interactions of smell, etc.)—are basically energy stimuli to

Figure 2.3 EOS, Sean Lally's 2014 project for the ongoing Istanbul Design Biennial, shows how energy can be used as an architectural building material. The hovering portable "suns" release energy to define gathering spaces with distinct light, heat and acoustic experiences.

our sensory systems (Figure 2.3). He describes this energy as consisting of gradient fields, building and subsiding in geometric formations. In his work, he uses these material energies as "building blocks" for defining spatial boundaries and shape.[16] He reminds us that although these material energies may appear to be more frail as building elements, they are also more nimble and able to change as needed.[17] Lally's approach helps us envision sensory envelopes that organize space and activities independently of the solid tectonic surfaces. And he reminds us: "The sensitivity of the body's sensory perception determines what it can identify as boundary limits within the environment. ... The extent to which those edges are identifiable determines how the body distinguishes one shape or threshold from another."[18] These variations of sensory gradients across a place are its *sensescape*, analogous to the landscape that charts the topographic variations of landforms.

Celebration of the Senses

As we envision three-dimensional sensescapes, we can start to recognize their physical features. Their three-dimensional volumetric shapes are defined by boundaries, gradients of sensation that may be abrupt or gradual depending on the way the sensory energy grows or dissipates. As we enter or leave sensory spaces, we may cross recognizable thresholds of sensation; or the change may be so subtle that we don't register the moment of transition. We may think of sensory spaces with gradual gradients as more "porous" than those with steep gradients. For example, as we enter an active plaza from a quiet side street leading straight into it, we may gradually experience the increase in sound level until we reach the crescendo of sound at its center. The increase in sound will depend on many things including the spread and directionality of the sound sources, how plaza surfaces reflect the sound, how walls and materials of side street surfaces funnel sound out of the plaza, how quickly we are walking, etc. In this instance, we may not recognize a clear threshold of entering or leaving the sound space. But entering the same plaza by abruptly turning a corner from a protected adjacent alley may suddenly and dramatically change the sound level from a background hum to a vibrant cacophony. So the topography of the soundscape may be gradual or abrupt, and the conscious shaping of these aural gradients becomes a new palette for the astute designer.

As we start to recognize characteristics of sensory topography, we will develop a language similar to that of tectonic space. We may identify alcoves or entire rooms of sound, light or odor. We will note their boundaries and their shapes. At the urban scale, we may create sensemarks—paths, nodes and intersections of sensory intensity. We may experience ourselves being inside or outside these sensory spaces and pass through portals or cross thresholds of sensory gradients. Our designs may celebrate these transitions, just as a rose-covered trellis that provides a gateway to a garden intensifies the olfactory gradient and creates an attention-grabbing threshold of aroma at the point of entry.

The sensory environments we create may be simple or complex. They may be patterned or repeat in a rhythmic progression, as when a regular, repeating street grid alternates a blast of cold wind at each intersection with the relatively protected calm at mid-block. Through our explorations of sensory space in this book, we will train our bodies to notice these rhythms around us. We will explore the simulation tools that help us predict and visualize their occurrence, and we will learn to consciously shape them in our designs.

One intriguing aspect of sensory space is the interaction of our bodies with it. We are sensory beings in a sensory world—inseparable from it. As we move into a thermal space, we bring our heat into it with us. Each of us is a 100-watt heater that contributes to the thermal ambience of the space. Similarly, we bring our sounds, both in the vocalizations that we make and in the intentional and unintentional interactions of our movements with the surfaces around us. The presence of people in a hard-edged room provides a softness that tempers the most austere setting. Our smells blend with the smells that surround us. So we are bodies immersed in a sensual world and we add our sensory inputs to it. It is a great interplay of sensory stimuli, an immersed sensing body, a remembering/naming mind and a cultural overlay of meaning. It is a rich, fluid field, and this text will provide us with ways to look at it through the lens of each of the senses.

But even these senses are not separate as they overlap with each other and intermingle in a synesthesia of experience. "Multidimensional space" is a term sometimes used to describe this overlapping of sensory spaces as it describes the depth of experience we encounter beyond the traditional three dimensions of tectonic space. Lisa Heschong addresses this as follows:

> "Since each sense contributes a slightly different perception of the world, the more senses involved in a particular experience, the fuller, the rounder, the experience becomes. If sight allows for a three-dimensional world, then each other sense contributes at least one, if not more, additional dimensions. The most vivid, most powerful experiences are those involving all of the senses at once."[19]

As we explore these sensory overlaps more in Chapter 8, we will see how sensory spaces that progress in a coherent way create an intensified node or path. The warmth and brightness of a window seat in sunlight is heightened by the placement of a fragrant flower in it. The excitement of a mall shopping experience builds as the sounds of people, the smells of bakeries, the lights of shops progress from entryway to central space, promising more to come around every corner. At the other extreme, we will see that when sensory spaces are mismatched, they create discordance that is sometimes perceived as a subtle statement about difference and sometimes as a playful or dramatic illusion.

RE-ENCHANTMENT OF THE WORLD

Ultimately, this work is about the love of place—truly being immersed in and experiencing place with our whole body. Our mind resides in the distant separation of vision, but our other senses require the intimate participation of body in place. We are of this world, intimately connecting with all of our senses. We are not stewards of an unsteady, failing ship; we are passengers on the deck, immersed in the journey. We must understand our world in this way— embracing all experiences and feeling our way back into the world with all our senses.

As designers, we cannot create a specific experience. We can't insure the feelings/thoughts/memories that will arise in a particular person. But we can orchestrate the occurrence and shape of the sensory inputs to create the possibility of experience. For the sensory environment is by its very nature a full-body experience, a feeling of being within. As Juhani Pallasmaa reminds us, "a meaningful building establishes a dialogue between itself and the occupant's body as well as his/her memory and mind."[20] In alignment with the current understanding of space versus place, the experience of the sensory realm is really an interaction between the sensory stimuli that exist within a place and its occupant(s). Churchill was being simplistic when he said, "We shape our buildings and afterwards our buildings shape us."[21] It is more an iterative process, a conversation as it were, among the existing characteristics of a place, the human interaction of shaping form and sensory experiences to alter that place (or a portion of it) and the dwelling that then happens and evolves within it. Over time, this conversation creates shared cultural experiences and understandings (meanings) of these shared places. Knowing place is an intricate (and personal) interaction between what is sensed and the entity that is sensing.[22]

So, like the beginning pianist, it is not enough to learn the individual notes to understand a symphony. We must sit under the dome of Salzburg Cathedral and feel the sound build around us. Thus, the real learning is to go out, immerse ourselves in sensory places and observe (Figure 2.4). As we do this, we must note how we feel; what

Celebration of the Senses

Figure 2.4 The real learning is to go out, immerse ourselves in sensory places and observe. Only by directly experiencing the sounds, aromas, textures, temperatures and light spaces around us can we truly know the sense of place they create.

memories, emotions and dreams are evoked; where we are drawn closer or repelled away. We must immerse ourselves in this full-body experience and carry this embodied knowledge forward into our future design processes.

For convenience, this book breaks down our perceptions by the common categories of our sensory systems (with small adjustments at times to reflect the process of design for the built environment). In each chapter, one of the senses is brought to the foreground for examination. In approaching our analysis in this way, we run the risk of being the doctors who kill the patient by dissection to diagnose the problem. As Lawrence Hass points out, "analytic understanding is useful and clarifying; but there is always more going on in experience, always more than any analysis can capture."[23] So as we move sequentially through the sensory fields, we must remember that the sense we are examining lives within an interactive background of other senses, other experiences, and that the whole of this interactive sensory field is larger than the mere sum of the pieces found within. We cannot truly speak of experiencing thermal space without the color and smell and sound within it. After we explore the senses one by one to reawaken our awareness to each of them, we will complete the process by honoring the unity of experience as we recombine them into a seamless and undifferentiated whole that is the sacred sense of place.

Notes

1   Gaston Bachelard, *The Poetics of Space*, translated by Maria Jolas, copyright © 1958 by Presses Universitaires de France; translation copyright © 1964 by the Orion Press Inc. Used by permission of Viking Books, an imprint of Penguin Publishing Group, a division of Penguin Random House LLC.
2   Christian Jarrett, *Great Myths of the Brain* (West Sussex: John Wiley & Sons, 2015), 238.
3   James Gibson cited in Kent C. Bloomer, and Charles W. Moore, *Body, Memory, and Architecture* (New Haven: Yale University Press, 1977), 33.
4   Lawrence Hass, *Merleau-Ponty's Philosophy* (Bloomington and Indianapolis: Indiana University Press, 2008), 33.
5   Ibid., 36.
6   Juhani Pallasmaa, "Body, mind and imagination: the mental essence of architecture," chapter 3 in *Mind in Architecture: Neuroscience, Embodiment and the Future of Design*, ed. Sarah Robinson and Juhani Pallasmaa (Cambridge: The MIT Press, 2015), 61.
7   Mark L. Johnson, "The embodied meaning of architecture," chapter 2 in *Mind in Architecture: Neuroscience, Embodiment and the Future of Design*, ed. Sarah Robinson and Juhani Pallasmaa (Cambridge: The MIT Press, 2015), 38–40.
8   Christian Norberg-Schulz, *Genius Loci: Towards a Phenomenology of Architecture* (New York: Rizzoli, 1980), 83.
9   Lisa Heschong, *Thermal Delight in Architecture* (Cambridge: The MIT Press, 1982), 33–5.
10 Juhani Pallasmaa, *The Eyes of the Skin: Architecture and the Senses* (West Sussex: John Wiley & Sons, 2005), 50.
11 Victoria Henshaw, *Urban Smellscapes: Understanding and Designing City Smell Environments* (New York: Routledge, 2014), 42–5.
12 Gaston Bachelard, *The Poetics of Space* (Boston: Beacon Press, 1969), 39.
13 Heschong, *Thermal Delight in Architecture*, 23.
14 Alliesthesia describes how a sensory stimulus may be perceived with either pleasure or disgust depending on the internal state of an organism. If a stimulus improves the internal state, it is perceived as pleasant; if it worsens the internal state, it is perceived as unpleasant or even painful. Sensations are

thus subjective and depend not only on the quality of the stimulus but also on the current state of internal receptors.

15 Jean-Charles Chebat and Richard Michon, "Impact of ambient odours on mall shoppers' emotions, cognition, and spending: a test of competitive causal theories," *Journal of Business Research* 56, no. 7 (July 2003), 529–39.

16 Sean Lally, *The Air from Other Planets: A Brief History of Architecture to Come* (Zurich: Lars Müller Publishers, 2013), 24.

17 Ibid., 225.

18 Ibid., 161.

19 Heschong, *Thermal Delight in Architecture*, 29.

20 Juhani Pallasmaa, *The Embodied Image: Imagination and Imagery in Architecture* (West Sussex: John Wiley & Sons, 2011), 43.

21 Prime Minister Winston Churchill, House of Commons debate on rebuilding, October 28, 1944.

22 Keith H. Basso, "Wisdom sits in places," chapter 2 in *Senses of Place*, ed. Steven Feld and Keith H. Basso (Santa Fe: School of American Research Press, 1996), 56.

23 Hass, *Merleau-Ponty's Philosophy*, 47.

Light Space

Chapter 3

"Someone asked what my favorite material was and I said, 'Light.' I really believe in a certain sense you can sculpt with light."[1]

Steven Holl

Seattle's change of seasons is marked less by falling temperatures than by a change in light. High summer sun gives way in winter to an amorphous luminous haze that has been called "oyster light" due to its shimmering pearlescence, reminiscent of the inside of an oyster shell.[2] Seattle's winter light is not brash and showy as it is in dry, sunny parts of the country, but is shy and retiring. When the sky is overcast, as often happens, daylight seeps around corners and pads its way tentatively under tables like a cat stalking a dust bunny. The space it creates is a spongy, moist entity that brightens periodically with the glow of an electric lamp or an errant ray of sunshine. It's a forgiving light, hiding flaws and blemishes, softening hard edges. It is very different from the light of Italy where the contrast between sunlight and shadow are so remarkably sharp that it led to the Renaissance notion of positive light space and negative shadow space alternating rhythmically across a building façade. I feel at home in Seattle because its light suits me. In stark sunshine, I feel awkward and exposed. I am not alone—Seattleites lean toward darker colors; tropical colors can look comically out of place, especially in winter. We are creatures of this soggy light, and we call it home for eight months of the year until the sun reappears in summer.

The quality and shape of light in a place sets its character. The flow of light spaces, as they change either gradually or abruptly, can draw us forward, make our hearts leap or speak of mystery and danger. The experience of light space is perhaps one of the easiest to understand. Like tectonic space, its immediate effects are experienced through sight, the predominant human sensory mode. Yet the phenomenological experience of being immersed in light is rarely discussed.

In *Becoming Animal*, David Abram whimsically captures this two-dimensional versus three-dimensional experience as he explores light's opposite, the realm of shadow. He notes that "one of the countless signs that our thinking minds have grown estranged from the intelligence of our sensing bodies, is that today a great many people seem to believe that shadows are flat."[3] To the contrary, on exploring his own shadow, Abram experiences

> "a precisely bounded zone of darkness that floats between my opaque flesh and that vaguely humanoid silhouette laid out upon the pavement. … The actual shadow does not reside primarily on the ground; it is a voluminous being of thickness and depth, a mostly unseen presence that dwells in the air *between* my body and that ground."[4]

Similarly, we see where light lands, but only when particles of dust or vapor are suspended in the air can we see the shape and volume of the light space itself. The rest of the time, we only subconsciously register this volume of light between the light source (whether it is the sun or an electric light) and the surfaces it illuminates. Yet, we experience entering and leaving light space all the time. We sense its boundaries, anticipating when we will move from light to shadow or the reverse. We take joy in the rhythm of walking down a tree-lined street, moving from sun to shadow on a cool spring day. We duck into a shadowed corner to be alone or spread our arms wide in an expansive field of sunshine. And with practice, we can learn the language and form of this magical light space.

IN THE BLINK OF AN EYE

Our understanding of light space requires a basic understanding of the mechanics of sight and the process of visual perception. Light is just the name we use for that portion of the electromagnetic spectrum to which our eyes are tuned. Although the spectrum is continuous, we divide it into segments based on how it is useful to us. The human eye sees electromagnetic energy with wavelengths between 390 and 700 nanometers (nm), a range corresponding to a color spectrum with violet at the shortest end and red at the longest.

Although other parts of our bodies respond to light, our eyes are the detectors that evolved for sight. Vision was the last and arguably the most specialized sense to be developed in humans. Sight gained dominance over smell when man's ancestors left the jungle floor and took to the trees, requiring keen vision to survive.[5] Like all of our sensory receivers, the human eye is a complex sensing device. Humans have camera-type eyes, as do many birds, reptiles and fish. Just as a camera lens focuses light onto film, two structures in the eye (the cornea and the lens) work together to focus light onto the retina, a light-sensitive membrane at the back of the eye. Situated between the cornea and the lens is the iris, a ring-shaped muscular tissue with an adjustable circular opening, called the pupil, that expands or contracts to adjust the amount of light entering the eye. This variable aperture allows us to function in widely different light levels—from romantically low moonlight to bright sunlight more than one million times more intense. But this adaptation response is not immediate and may take several minutes (even longer as we age), during which time we have difficulty seeing, being blinded by either too much light or too little.

Light rays that reach the retina through the pupil strike millions of light-sensitive cells—cones and rods—embedded in its surface. Cones are centralized on the retina and are specialized to detect color and visual sharpness. They dominate vision in the center of our visual field (the innermost 2 degrees) and operate best at high light levels. Rods, on the other hand, are distributed more toward the outer rim of the retina where they contribute to our peripheral vision (a wider cone of vision of about 170 degrees).[6] Rods register only black and white information, dominate vision at very low light levels, and are especially sensitive to motion and bright/dark contrasts. Their function in peripheral vision is important to our orientation and experience of immersion within a sensory world. Juhani Pallasmaa notes this viscerally in *The Eyes of the Skin* where he points out: "Focused vision confronts us with the world whereas peripheral vision envelops us in the flesh of the world. … Peripheral vision integrates us with space, while focused vision pushes us out of the space, making us mere spectators."[7]

These specialized roles of cones and rods worked together for the survival of our species. Rods were the first to signal when something was approaching quickly from the periphery, and as we turned our heads toward it, the cones sharply identified whether it was friend or foe. Thus the rods served as watchdogs for imminent danger at the periphery. It is this primal tension, still active within us, that adds to the excitement of strobe lights in a dance club or that triggers a stress reaction to overhead flickering lights in a work environment.

Once light strikes the rods and cones, it is converted into electric signals that are relayed to the brain via the optic nerve. The brain decodes these signals into the images a person sees, comparing the images received by our two eyes to provide information about spatial depth and our location in space relative to other objects.

Thus visual perception depends on the characteristics of four things: the light source (the color wavelengths it contains and its intensity), the reflecting object (its reflection, absorption and transmission of different wavelengths), the sensing eye, and the brain processing the information within the context of all that is around it. The apparent brightness of a space or object depends on all of these. So there are several ways to measure light in a space. The easiest one to record and understand is the intensity of the light that falls on an object or surface. The units of this measurement are footcandles (fc); one footcandle is equivalent to the illumination produced by one candle at a distance of one foot. The metric unit is the lux (lx; equivalent to 0.093 fc). Many lighting standards are based on a minimum value for this illumination on a work surface. For example, many school classroom designs in the United States require a minimum of 30 fc (323 lx) of light on the desktops.

However, unless we are lying on a desktop looking up at the light, our eyes don't see this incident light, only the light that reflects back off the surfaces around us. So a better way to measure light in a place is to determine the amount and distribution of this reflected light. Consider, for example, two alcoves, one painted white and one painted dark brown, which are illuminated with the same amount of light (Figures 3.1 and 3.2). The white alcove glows with reflected light, while the brown one absorbs most of the light and creates a darker, more private setting even though they both initially receive the same illumination. Since this second measure of reflected light combines information about both the amount and direction of light and the reflecting surfaces, it more accurately depicts how we experience light in a space. These luminance (brightness) distributions or ratios are also factored in by lighting designers and more sophisticated lighting codes.

The distribution of light and dark areas catches our eyes as we look around a space. But as we scan the surroundings, our eyes don't slide across features in a continuous steady movement. Instead, they jump from one

Figures 3.1 and 3.2 When this library alcove is painted white, the walls reflect most of the incoming daylight, creating a bright, open appearance. When painted dark brown, on the other hand, the walls absorb most of the light, making the space feel smaller and more intimate.

point of interest to the next in an erratic pattern like the ball in a pinball machine. These jumps are called saccadic eye movements, and they can be followed experimentally with precision eye tracking devices to show the progression of a person's eye as it scans a particular scene. When the resulting spiderweb of trails is superimposed on a photograph of the scene, it shows the nodes of interest where the eye has paused to take in information. From these studies, scientists have determined the hierarchy of things that attract our eyes. Two important attractions for survival are the features of a person's face and quick movements in space. Our eyes are also drawn to spots of brightness, edges with high contrast, vivid colors and strong patterns.[8] So our eyes are actually seeking rather than just passively collecting information.

All of these findings reflect an allure with strong signals and contrast between opposites, which is common across all the senses. Contrast, usually described as a ratio of the measured brightness (luminance) of light to dark surfaces, depends on both the light delivered to the space and the surface reflectance of objects in the space. Brightness contrast can thus be generated by varying the light levels across the space and/or varying the reflectance of objects and surfaces. Both of these actions create texture in the lit environment and help our peripheral vision provide orientation and spatial perception.[9] Too little contrast makes a space flat and uninteresting; too much creates distraction or glare.

Unfortunately in many modern buildings, especially work environments, this richness of lighting design is neglected in deference to the goals of standardization and flexibility. In the vast majority of commercial buildings, the architect finishes the spatial design and then hands it off to an engineer who lays out the lighting in a standardized grid in the dropped ceiling to deliver a uniform light level throughout the building. As noted in Chapter 1, this use of uniform light levels gained popularity in the mid-twentieth century with the rise of fluorescent lighting and the promise of electrical energy that would supply all our needs with power that was "too cheap to meter."

But this new approach also had its critics. In *A Pattern Language*, Christopher Alexander et al. didn't mince words when they remarked: "Uniform illumination—the sweetheart of the lighting engineers—serves no useful purpose whatsoever. In fact, it destroys the social nature of space, and makes people feel disoriented and unbounded."[10] What we gained in flexibility, we lost in interest and delight. Although these uniformly lit spaces are egalitarian, the light they provide creates no special places that draw us together. The poetic champion of sensory space, Gaston Bachelard, poignantly lamented this loss, noting: "The evening lamp on the family table is also the center of a world. In fact, the lamp-lighted table is a little world in itself, and a dreamer-philosopher may well fear lest our indirect lighting cause us to lose the center of the evening room"[11] (Figure 3.3).

About the same time that Alexander et al. were voicing their concerns in the 1970s, most major industrial countries of the world were also experiencing an energy crisis. Rather than being too cheap to meter, power prices skyrocketed. Conservation became the watchword, and in response the lighting profession promoted a three-tiered approach with separate standards for task, accent and ambient lighting. Light levels were reduced for background ambient lighting, which still blanketed spaces in relatively uniform light levels, but the addition of task lighting and accent lighting increased light levels where they were needed to perform focused work or to highlight

Figure 3.3 The glow of light around a dining table centers the space and creates a cozy gathering node separated from the larger room by light alone.

art and architectural features. This was an important initial step toward the differentiation of light levels, but its pragmatic premise stopped short of exploring the full phenomenological potential of light space. As we explore the world of light, shadow, color and pattern space in the sections that follow, we'll delve more deeply into the volumetric qualities of light that capture the desire of Bachelard's dreamer-philosopher for light spaces that are little worlds unto themselves.

THE SHAPE OF LIGHT

Originating in the theater lighting profession, lighting design has long carried the power to create mini-environments within a larger setting. Just as a theater spotlight defines a small cone of activity within the larger stage, so creative architectural lighting can generate light spaces that feel separated from the space around them. It is exactly this that makes the oculus of the Pantheon so captivating (Figure 3.4). Though it's just a simple circular opening to the sky, the finger of light it creates traces its way across the coffered surfaces of the Pantheon's hemispheric

Figure 3.4 At the Pantheon, a finger of light traces its way across interior coffered surfaces, at times reaching down to the floor to create a column of light connecting visitors with the oculus above.

interior, independent from it and yet intimately connected—predictable and yet mystical. When it touches down to the floor, the urge to stand in its spotlight is compelling. We are pulled to experience that ephemeral space, singled out by light alone as if on a stage within the greater whole.

Some light spaces occur naturally, such as the cozy glow of a window seat in direct sunlight or the shady recess beneath a willow tree. Others are more intentionally designed. As our buildings open to the sun, they admit volumes of light shaped by the openings in them and their orientation toward the sun. Electric lighting may also shape light space with carefully controlled light distribution. Even a simple streetlight carves a volume of safety out of the darkness. Good lighting designers use both daylight and electric lighting to craft light spaces not confined by physical walls. They create glowing spheres of light around restaurant tables to envelop intimate diners. They entice us with glimpses of bright volumes of light bulging out from behind walls or produce a dazzling pavilion of light to celebrate the intersection of two long hallways. In each of these, with practice we can sense when we have entered and left the light space, how intense it is, and how porous or abrupt its boundaries appear.

Lighting designers think about lighting in terms of sources (that generate the light), fixtures (the entities that shape and distribute light to the space) and surfaces (that redistribute the light throughout the space). The source may be natural, like sunlight or the overcast skylight, or an electrically generated "artificial" source. Sources are categorized by how they distribute light, either as a point or diffuse source. Point sources are considered to have negligible dimensions so that they can be easily focused and manipulated. Incandescent, metal halide and many LED lamps are common forms of point source. The sun, although quite large, is also considered a point source because its distance from the Earth creates light rays on the Earth's surface that are highly aligned (parallel) and thus act like a focused point source. When point sources are focused, they create sharp shadows and high relief as they illuminate objects or buildings in the environment. They provide an abrupt transition between light and shadow. They also create glittering highlights in specular reflective surfaces like polished brass and cut glass. This combination of sharp shadows and sparkling surfaces brings depth and drama and can make the light space dance with life around its occupants.

Diffuse sources, on the other hand, provide a flat, directionless light that can't be easily focused. They generate diffuse shadows that soften the edges of objects, people and architectural features. Fluorescent lamps are diffuse sources, providing a soft glow of light from the phosphors coating the inside surface of the lamp. Any point source that reflects off or shines through a diffusing surface will be transformed into a diffuse source. Both the overcast sky and the blue skylight are natural diffuse sources. Diffuse sources tend to fill a space with light, creating a sense of largeness and openness.

A light source combined with a light fixture is called a luminaire, and it is the performance of this entire system that determines how light is delivered to a space. When daylight is the light source, the whole building acts as the luminaire, shaping the distribution of daylight in the space. The design of luminaires determines which building volumes receive light, which of their surfaces receive light directly from the source and which ones receive only reflected light. The surfaces in turn have properties of reflectance, absorption and transmission that determine how they hold the light. They may let it freely pass through (as glass and translucent materials do), absorb most of it (as dark-colored surfaces do), or reflect it either specularly (like a mirror) or diffusely (like matte white surfaces) around the space to fill the space with light.

Because we can't actually see the light space (unless there is a vapor in the air), when we enter a space, we use surface information to gauge the shape, size and intensity of the light spaces it contains. Some of these light spaces accommodate a large or small group of people; others may only highlight a small piece of art. Some may turn off or dim at the command of an electric light switch or the drawing of a curtain; others fluctuate with the natural rhythm of the regional climate or time of day.

THE LIGHT OF PLACE

As Seattle's oyster light demonstrates, each region has unique qualities of light that imbue its city streets, buildings and landscape with its own quirky luminous personality, which may be somber, cheerful, erratic, ethereal, fierce or mysterious.

Near the equator, noontime sun beats straight down on the roofs of buildings throughout the year. Shadows pool at the base of trees, and small overhangs are sufficient to shade a full building elevation. Seasonal differences are minor; the sun's rays are bright and intense year-round, especially where there is little moisture in the air. Buildings and streets huddle under multiple layers of shade (Figures 3.5 and 3.6).

As we move toward the poles at higher latitudes, the sun slides lower in the sky, shadows lengthen and sunlight flows more laterally into buildings. Low sun angles lengthen the path of solar rays through the Earth's atmosphere, scattering the light so that by the time it

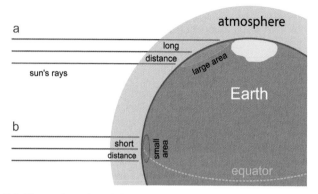

Figure 3.5 The quality of sunlight varies with the latitude of the site. At higher latitudes, sunlight arrives at low angles, is weakened by its long transit through Earth's atmosphere and casts long shadows. Near the equator, sunlight is often directly overhead, travels a short distance through the atmosphere, casts short shadows and is more intense.

arrives at the Earth's surface, it is a pale and feeble ghost of its former self. Seasons are dramatically differentiated. Daylight hours in summer stretch from early morning to late at night; in winter, they shorten to a few precious hours or disappear altogether. Sunlight is a cherished commodity. Buildings are designed to reach for it, spread it around and hoard it (Figure 3.7).

For all latitudes, local seasonal climates determine the air moisture level, which in turn affects the preponderance of direct sun or overcast skies and determines the cloud patterns (whether they are puffy and high or heavy and low) and how they scatter light. The dryness/humidity determines the clarity of the light and the sharpness of its shadows. As air moisture and overcast skies prevail, daylight diffuses and shadows soften. The local geography too plays a part in shaping the light of a place, determining how open it is to the sky. The unobstructed horizon of the plains region in the United States is capped by a sky that hovers like a large blue bowl over the land, while deep Alpine valleys chop the sky into narrow slots of

Light Space

Figure 3.6 Near the equator, sunlight is intense and sun penetration into buildings is avoided. Windows in these traditional residences in Yemen are intricately shaded, creating cool and dark interiors with only sparkles of sunlight animating the window plane.

Figure 3.7 At higher latitudes, the feeble rays of the sun are welcomed into buildings. These traditional residences in Amsterdam respond with large windows reaching to the top of high ceilings to create interior spaces flooded with daylight.

blue, limiting the land's sun exposure to just a handful of hours a day. In a similar way, the dense city streets of New York and Shanghai create urban canyons with little access to direct sunlight. In turn, these solar patterns attract complementary plants and trees that filter the light in specific ways that further come to characterize the place. All these factors establish the regional hue for the rich palette of daylight that the architect or urban planner works with. To this, the designer then overlays electric lighting to augment daylight when it's not available.

THE PLACE OF LIGHT

Lighting designers envision lighting designs in a variety of different ways. One of the design frameworks that most closely touches on the concept of light space as a volumetric element is also one of the oldest. Richard Kelly, often revered as the father of lighting design, envisioned three areas of light energy impacts: focal glow, ambient luminescence and play of brilliants. Focal glow (Figure 3.8) is a localized area of light surrounded by relative darkness. Kelly poetically describes it as:

> "the campfire of all time … the pool of light at your favorite reading chair … the shaft of sunshine that warms the far end of the valley. … Focal glow draws attention … separates the important from the unimportant."[12]

When we are within the focal glow, we are within the center—Bachelard's "little world in itself." This is the type of light space that is created when each table in a romantic restaurant is lit with a single candle or an electric light centered above it, leaving the space between tables comparatively dark. Each set of diners occupies their own individual area of focal glow. Their place is special and this importance is not diminished by the fact that every other table is also special.

Figure 3.8 The use of focal glow at St. Henry's Ecumenical Art Chapel by Sanaksenaho Architects (2005) draws our attention to the altar.

Light Space

Figure 3.9 Denver International Airport's tensile roof provides ambient luminescence to evenly light the expansive terminal spaces (Fentress Architects, 1995).

Ambient luminescence, on the other hand, fills a whole space with a large volume of light (Figure 3.9). Kelly said that ambient luminescence is like

> "the uninterrupted light of a snowy morning in the open country. It is foglight at sea in a small boat, it is twilight gaze on a wide river where shore and water and sky are indistinguishable. … Ambient luminescence produces shadowless illumination. It minimizes form and bulk. It minimizes the importance of all things. … It suggests the freedom of space and can suggest infinity."[13]

Ambient luminescence is characterized by diffuse lighting schemes, and although it can be overused, it can also create a calm container for the hectic activities within it.

Figure 3.10 Pendant lights drop like stars into the main sanctuary of Myyrmäki Church by Juha Leiviskä (Helsinki, 1984), providing a play of brilliants against a backdrop of soft, diffuse daylight.

Play of brilliants is the sparkle of lights that occurs when we directly see a series of small point sources or when a point source is scattered off a reflective surface (Figure 3.10). For this, Kelly calls to mind

"Times Square at night. It is the eighteenth century ballroom of crystal chandeliers and many candle flames ... sunlight on a fountain or a rippling brook ... the rose window of Chartres ... a sparkling cabinet of fine glassware. ... Play of brilliants stimulates the body and spirit, quickens the appetite, awakens curiosity. ... It is distracting or entertaining."[14]

A play of brilliants requires point sources, often sprinkled around a light space defined by focal glow or ambient luminescence, to give it life and animation. So, for example, strings of twinkling lights may be used overhead to create a ceiling plane that hovers above and bounds a specific area of a plaza at night, or they may be scattered randomly around a holiday mall to add a festive glimmer to the ambient daylight.

Kelly's format focuses on the overall ambiance of light in a space, while the task/accent/ambient trilogy mentioned earlier deals more with the functions that light performs to facilitate work and promote comfort and safety within a space. These are two different and important perspectives on generating both useable and inspirational light spaces. All of these light impacts take their place within the three-dimensional frame of the built environment, and as Marietta Millet reminds us,

> "It seems an obvious statement that light emphasizes form. The truth is that sometimes it does and sometimes it does not. A form in light may be there in our visual field, but that does not necessarily mean that we see it clearly or in the way intended."[15]

Sometimes the light and the tectonic forms exactly overlap and read as a single light/tectonic volume. At other times, light space flows independently of the physical surfaces.

Light is wonderfully fluid and may be used to either emphasize or dematerialize form and materials. Light reinforces the form of a space when it evenly illuminates the bounding surfaces. If the surfaces are light and reflective, they activate our peripheral vision and we feel immersed within the light space. Bright and even illumination of the ceiling makes it read as a whole, continuous surface, creating Kelly's ambient luminescence. This may also cause it to appear higher. Uniformly lighting the walls also makes a place feel more spacious. Light acts to dematerialize form when it does not match the spatial layout or when it creates such high contrast that parts of the visual field recede into darkness. The distribution of focal glow within a space determines its feeling of symmetry and balance independent of the regularity of its geometric form. Lighting from only one side creates asymmetry and suggests mystery (Figure 3.11). Lighting designers may even intentionally use light to camouflage a room's geometric shape. For example, a designer may intentionally lower the apparent height of a room by using pendant lights to create a layer of light below the actual ceiling height.

Lighting that accentuates structural elements makes them appear more robust, reinforcing their significance in shaping built form. For example, using uplighting on arches to exaggerate their height and form reinforces their role as defining elements of the building's structure and presence. At the material scale, lighting aimed at a low angle grazes surfaces, exaggerating texture and giving great depth and solidity. Higher-angle, diffuse light can make surfaces appear less substantial or even ephemeral.

Light may also work to either unify or disconnect adjacent spaces. Light flowing from one space to another tends to connect the two spaces, while an abrupt change in light level separates them. The degree of separation established by the light difference can set the tone for a transition from outside to inside a building. A transition from a bright exterior environment to a dark interior exaggerates the experience of enclosure and separation from the outside. On the other hand, if the interior is bright, admitting daylight freely across its space, the transition is minimized and may almost disappear if the daylight is combined with large exterior views.

Figure 3.11 A side window at St. Hallvard Church by Lund + Slaatto (Oslo, 1966) provides grazing light that creates a sense of mystery and accentuates the texture of the adjacent brick wall.

Light is important in setting spatial hierarchies and directing movement. We have noted how a pool of light with darker space surrounding it focuses attention. The brightest node is usually perceived as the most important; areas with low illumination diminish in their significance. Since people are phototropic (tending to move toward the light),[16] a node of light at an entrance or intersection or leaking out around a corner may draw people toward it, adding a directional flow to the experience of the space.

DESIGNING THE DARK

Darkness is the shadow side of light space. If light spaces are to take form, they require shadow spaces to hold them. As Pallasmaa reminds us, "in great architectural spaces, there is a constant, deep breathing of shadow and light; shadow inhales and illumination exhales light."[17] Although darkness is often considered the background from which the light spaces emerge, shadow spaces too should be intentionally designed as places of intimacy and refuge. Areas of darkness give texture to light space. At the smallest scale, this texture shows up as fine-grained pockets of shadow on the surface of a material grazed with light. At a larger scale, shadow texture appears as negative light spaces clinging to the shadow sides of objects or as three-dimensional volumes of darkness nestled among three-dimensional volumes of light.

Tanizaki's essay *In Praise of Shadows* is a homage to the magic of the dark. Exploring the mystery of the *tokonoma*, he muses,

> "A Japanese room might be likened to an inkwash painting, the paper-paneled shoji being the expanse where the ink is thinnest, and the alcove where it is darkest. Whenever I see the alcove of a tastefully built Japanese room, I marvel at our comprehension of the

secrets of shadows, our sensitive use of shadow and light. … Where lies the key to this mystery? Ultimately it is the magic of shadows. Were the shadows to be banished from its corners, the alcove would in that instant revert to mere void."[18]

The sensitive difference he notes here between the tectonic form of void and the enchantment of shadow space created by the alcove is an exquisite recognition of shaped light space.

Outside our buildings, we think about light and darkness in two different ways: the daytime experience of a world dominated by light and animated by pockets of darkness where the sunlight does not reach; and the nighttime experience of a world of darkness probed by fingers of light. Everything we erect on Earth casts a shadow upon the land. Just as the sun orients us toward the equator, its shadows point us toward the Earth's polar axes. As we have seen, the sun's shadows carry subtle information about time and place. A shadow's length reminds us of the time of year and the latitude where we dwell; its direction tells us the time of day. Shadows also withhold the sun's warming rays from areas adjacent to our buildings. So in design, we think about where the volume of a building's shadow will appear throughout the day and in the different seasons of a year. Out of concern for solar access, Ralph Knowles, researcher and professor emeritus at the University of Southern California, promoted the concept of a solar envelope that would assure solar access to properties surrounding a given site. Software developed by his team locates the biggest container of space that would not cast shadows off a site between specified times of the day.[19]

At night, design concerns focus more on how light probes the dark world. Issues concern safety, the ecological impacts on animal behavior and trespass of light to the night sky. Lighting designer Linnaea Tillett addressed these issues in her sensitive design for St. Patrick's Island Park in Calgary, Canada.

"We not only designed the lighting; we designed the dark. We had to account for what different species need at night. Humans want ease of passage, i.e. enough light to see without nocturnal eyesight. Eagles, owls, bats and other fauna expect darkness and ever-changing moonlight. Here are some ways we approached this issue: Path lighting is limited to primary routes, with fixtures carefully shielded and narrowly focused—the immediate surrounding area dark. Winter recreation areas for skating, sledding and ice-skating are illuminated for after-dark play with controlled lighting that is only used when needed. Most of the park is kept dark."[20]

The ability of light and shadow to shape space, whether interior or exterior, has fascinated mankind since the earliest architectural works. A number of wonderful books explore this realm of design in detail, and readers who wish to pursue this in more depth are encouraged to make use of this wealth of accumulated wisdom.[21]

COLOR SPACE

Color brings another dimension to the experience of light/shadow space (Figure 3.12). Throughout a day, we make many decisions based on color. The ripeness of fruit, the health of a person or the mood of a room are all evaluated based on color differences. A single color is like a single musical note—it only has meaning relative to other colors. These meanings may be symbolic, spatial, synesthetic and emotional.

Since we see objects because of the light they reflect, in order for us to see an object of a particular color, the light

Figure 3.12 When Monumenta invited internationally renowned artist Daniel Buren to transform the Nave of the Grand Palais, he created *Excentrique(s): Work In Situ* (2012). In this work, visitors are invited to move through cylindrical rooms of color.

source must have that color of light in it and the object's surface characteristics must be such that they reflect that wavelength of light toward our eyes. Many light sources, like the sun, contain wavelengths across the entire visible color spectrum. When all frequencies are mixed together, we see what we call white light. If a red apple is illuminated with light that contains a red component, it will reflect the red light and absorb most other colors so that we will see it as a shade of red. But if it is illuminated by a light that has no red wavelengths, then the apple will absorb all the incident light and will appear grey or black. In the name of energy efficiency, some parking lots are lit with low-pressure sodium lamps that produce only a narrow spike of yellow light at a wavelength around 589 nm. In this light, all cars appear muddy shades of grey/brown, making it difficult to tell them apart visually (and making us grateful for our car remote clickers!).

Luckily, most of the light around us contains a wide range of color wavelengths. What we call white light is actually composed of a balance of wavelengths across the color spectrum, and that balance may lean toward the yellow or blue end of the spectrum. Consider the relative yellowness of sunlight compared to the blueish-grey light of an overcast sky. This difference is called the correlated color temperature (CCT) of the source and is expressed in degrees Kelvin (K). Contrary to a thermal scale, we call low color temperatures (below 3,200 K) "warm" because of their relative yellowness and high color temperatures (above 4,000 K) "cool" because of their relative blueness. Every light source can be assigned a color temperature, and many electric lamps show a color temperature specification on their packaging. Sometimes this appears as a general description as either warm white or cool white, but often a particular value for color temperature is given in degrees Kelvin. For example, most incandescent lamps have a color temperature of 2,700 K and appear rather yellowish compared to fluorescent light or daylight. Some lamps, like LED and fluorescent, can be purchased in a wide range from 2,700 K to 7,000 K. The color temperature of daylight depends on its source. Sunlight is about 4,800 K, which appears yellowish relative to the overcast sky at about 6,000 K and the blue sky at over 10,000 K. If we pay attention, we can see these subtle differences. For example, looking at a white wall, we may notice that a "warm white" (2,900 K) LED table lamp provides a golden glow compared to the daylight from an adjacent window. People have different preferences for color temperature and these sometimes depend on the situation. Studies have shown that people tend to prefer warmer color temperatures (around 2,700 K to 3,000 K) for lower light levels and more intimate settings, but cooler color temperatures (3,500 K to 4,000 K) for workspaces and more active settings.

Although light at high and low color temperatures will shift how we see specific colors (lower color temperatures emphasize warm or red tones and higher color temperatures blue tones), another characteristic of lamps, the color rendering index (CRI), is much more significant in describing how true colors will appear under a particular light source. The CRI is a number from 0 to 100 that represents each light source's ability to accurately render eight standard color samples.[22] Lower numbers represent poorer color rendering performance. Both daylight and incandescent light have a CRI equal to 100. Most other electric sources have lower CRIs, ranging from the low 50s to 100. Lamps with a low CRI, like the early versions of fluorescent lamps, distort or dull colors and make skin tones look unnatural. Both CRI and color temperature significantly affect how comfortable people feel in a place. The lighting designers for the Los Angeles Lakers' STAPLES Center basketball arena took this to heart when they selected the new LED lighting. In addition to improving the energy efficiency, they also optimized the color temperature and CRI to make the yellow and purple of the Lakers' uniforms "pop" for spectators and TV monitors.[23]

Color vision starts with cones on the retina, but color perception happens in the brain. Experiments have shown that humans can distinguish between 2.3 million and 7.5 million colors.[24] What we see and the colors we experience may be heavily distorted by our brains to match our expectations. In fact, our brains are programmed to see the dominant light as white even if it is tinged with color. Note, for example, how yellow-tinted ski goggles make snow appear yellow at first, but this effect is neutralized over a short period of wearing them. This is the basis of many visual optical illusions. We sometimes see colors which are not there as an after-flash or a glow around the edges of a form due to cones which have become fatigued from focusing on their complementary color too long. We also misjudge colors and brightness levels to keep them consistent with our understanding of the environment. For example, we understand that a surface is the same color even though it appears brighter when it's facing the light source. This is known as color constancy, and it can be used to create interesting illusions (see Chapter 8).

Color space modifies haptic/textural space at both the micro and macro levels. At the micro level, it dissolves the surface of a wall when layers of semitransparent color give microscopic depth to the surface, making it appear less certain, less definitive. At the macro level, it may move architectural planes forward and back in our perceptual experience. Lois Swirnoff, following on the work of Josef Albers, conducted extensive research on our common perceptual assumptions about color space. Noting that many designers use color merely as an arbitrary embellishment, Swirnoff explored color's ability to shape space, enhance or diminish volume, and alter the apparent position of an object in space.[25] Her work demonstrates that most people experience red surfaces as advancing toward the viewer and blue surfaces as receding (Figure 3.13). Thus dark red surfaces diminish the perceived size of space, while light blue ones may increase it. Generally, cool, desaturated and light colors are considered to increase the experienced spaciousness, whereas warm, saturated and dark colors tend to have opposite effect. Darker, saturated color objects also tend to appear heavier. Obviously, these are simplifications

Figure 3.13 At Casa Gilardi (Mexico, 1976), Luis_Barragán's use of a red wing wall exaggerates its position in front of the blue wall that recedes to the back.

of color impacts, since all colors change their character when modified according to their lightness factor (light to dark) and saturation. But they serve to illustrate the impact color may have on the perception of physical space. Complementary colors create dynamic, "charged" edges when they appear adjacent to each other. Like a magician, the colorist can make us look at certain places while avoiding others, all beneath our conscious direction.

James Turrell uses color and light to create both works of art and contemplative gathering places. Sometimes his work consists of virtual or real alcoves of colored light that recede into a wall; at other times, his colored volumes project into the room, creating virtual objects and walls hovering so realistically in space that people have been known to try to lean against them. He also works with natural light to create Skyspaces—enclosures with an oculus opening to the sky.

The edge of the opening is tapered on the top side so that it appears as though its rim has no thickness. The resulting circular view of the sky revealed through the opening seems to float in the ceiling of the space, changing with the daylight conditions—sometimes a thin disc and, at other times, a bulbous egg of color. *The Color Inside*, Turrell's 84th Skyspace, sited on the campus of the University of Texas at Austin, is an elliptical structure of white plaster (Figures 3.14 and 3.15). During sunrise and sunset, colored lights illuminate its walls with a sequence of changing colors that crawl up the eggshell-like interior toward the oval oculus, revealing a mesmerizing depth and contrast of color space. At other times of the day, the Skyspace, lit only by daylight, offers a quiet, contemplative space.

In addition to affecting our perception of tectonic form, color impacts our moods and other sensory perceptions. Studies show that red excites people and makes them feel warmer, and it makes a space sound louder. Blue tends to make people calmer and less tolerant of cold and makes a space seem quieter. Pastel yellow is perceived as sunny, friendly and soft.[26] We crave some interest and variety of colors in our environments. A monotonous color palette with weak intensities of colors, monochromatic harmonies and low color contrasts sends weak environmental signals. The blandness creates an understimulated environment and may cause irritability and restlessness. On the other hand, overstimulation can result from highly saturated colors, color contrasts that are too complex or incongruous, or too many complex visual color patterns. These run the risk of increasing stress as indicated by increases in breathing rate, pulse rate, blood pressure and muscle tension.[27]

All of these impacts are layered upon geographic and cultural preferences for color in the environment, which

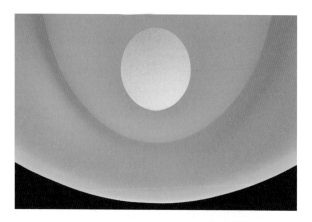

Figures 3.14 and 3.15 During sunrise and sunset (top), a sequence of color-changing lights illuminate James Turrell's Skyspace *The Color Inside*. The view of the sky through its oculus changes with the effects—at times, seeming like a floating disc of color and, at other times, appearing to project into or out of the aperture. During the daytime (bottom), the Skyspace, lit only by daylight, offers a quiet, contemplative space (James Turrell, Austin, 2013).

are often related to the daylight characteristics of a region. For example, we find that in more northern climates where sunlight is softer, cultures seem to prefer pale colors. Near the equator, on the other hand, the preference is for bold colors that will not be washed out by the strong sunlight there. Thus, rather than being a mere stylized overlay on our designs, color adds a dimensional depth to light space that is spatial, emotional, geographical and cultural.

PATTERN SPACE

Pattern space is an attribute of all the sensory spaces. It is the repeated change from one sensory experience to another and then back again. It may happen with light space as a series of pools of light from equally spaced streetlights punctuates a night streetscape, or it may happen with color space as a checkerboard pattern of colors follows us down a hallway. In all of these, we experience the rhythmic or arrhythmic appearance/ disappearance of a sensory signal and note its change across distance or time. In sound, we may orchestrate these rhythmic changes into musical meaning. In touch, it becomes texture. In a similar way we can experience the texture of light or of smell. Pattern is the rhythm of the light/dark, the yellow/blue, the high/low, the warm/cold, the sound/silence of our sensory world.

For light space, we depend on pattern to give us information about distance and progress and the coherence of surfaces. Both color fields and shade/ shadow patterns can break up an otherwise continuous surface into a multitude of fragments. For example, at the Seattle Central Library, direct sunlight shining through the structural grid creates a vibrant sun and shadow pattern on the floor of the adjacent reading room (Figure 3.16).

Figure 3.16 Sunlight through the heavily articulated structure at the Seattle Central Library creates a vibrant shadow pattern on the floor of the adjacent reading room (Rem Koolhaas and Joshua Prince-Ramus of OMA/ LMN, 2004).

REFLECTION SPACE

Because specular reflected light preserves apparent spatial information as a mirror image, it too changes the way we experience light space. We are all familiar with the technique of using mirrors in a small space to make that space appear larger because the reflections mask our perception of the bounding walls. Similarly, in an urban context, the use of reflective glazing can reduce the apparent scale of a building under certain daylight conditions (Figure 3.17). Thus, through reflection, light can make walls appear to move away from us or make them change character or disappear altogether. Although these

Figure 3.17
Reflections can camouflage tectonic form and/or make a place feel more expansive.

are all illusions of light space, they affect our perception and comfort in the places we inhabit.

SEEING THE LIGHT

We have seen how the experience of light space can have a powerful impact on our perception of place. It's important, therefore, for us to be able to anticipate these effects as we design new spaces. The most valuable tool for doing this is experience. There is no substitute for being in a place and being attuned to the light spaces around us, noting how our bodies feel as we move around, where we are tempted to linger, where we are drawn forward, whether we feel quieted or energized, private or social, how the light interacts with other sensory feelings. All good design starts with experience.

As we then attempt to recreate the experience in new designs, there are a number of different tools that can help simulate the experience. Most lighting simulation is done either with a physical scale model or a computer simulation. Less often, a portion of a space is constructed at full size so that an occupant can experience the true feeling in advance of the building's construction.

Even with the advent of computerized simulations, using a physical scale model to represent daylight in a space is still fairly common. If a model is built correctly, daylight interacts with the model in the same way it would in the full-size building; so it provides a good representation of how the light might feel, especially if a micro video camera is available to record the experience within the model space. Daylighting scale models are similar to the scale models that are common in architectural representation, but they are frequently larger (a scale of 1:50 up to 1:10) and are constructed with materials that have reflection and transmission characteristics similar to the materials that will be used in the final project. Daylight models are usually studied under an artificially simulated overcast sky or sun to eliminate the changeability of these conditions outdoors. However, they can also be viewed outdoors. Electrically lit scale models are less common because it is more difficult to scale the exact performance of a miniaturized light fixture. Several excellent resources are available to guide designers in constructing and evaluating scale models for lighting design.[28]

Because of the ease of integration with other design tools, computerized lighting simulations are being utilized more and more to simulate both daylight and electric light for interior or exterior built spaces. Although most CAAD and rendering programs have the ability to simulate some shade and shadow patterns from daylight in a space, not all programs can accurately predict the intensity and quality of the light space. In order to do this for daylight, a program must be able to represent a variety of sky conditions and the size, orientation and transmission characteristics of the building's windows and openings. For electric lighting, the program must accept the photometric properties of the luminaire, including its intensity and light distribution in all directions. For both types of simulations, the program must also be able to faithfully reproduce the reflections of light off surfaces in the space. If a program has these capabilities, the design team can obtain information about light levels and distribution in the space and may even be able to generate a virtual reality tour of the experience.

LIGHT PLAY

Light is one of the more evocative and playful sensory features of the world around us. Since the time of the Pyramids and Stonehenge, people have constructed monuments to celebrate the sun and chart its path. The predictability of the sun's movement across the sky allows "special effects" to be designed, taking advantage of solar angles on specific times of the day or year. The sundial is one of the more common manifestations of this, but other, more whimsical examples abound. For example, the phenomenon affectionately known as MIThenge marks the times of the year when the setting sun pokes its finger all the way down the length of MIT's Infinite Corridor, which runs from the main entrance on Massachusetts Avenue through Buildings 7, 3, 10, 4 and 8. When this happens, sunlight is projected down the full length of the corridor, a distance of 825 ft (251 m), and students and faculty line up to photograph and celebrate the event.[29]

Like Kelly's play of brilliants, these artistic and playful manipulations of daylight create an effect of beauty or whimsy that catches our eye and reminds us of the temporal or transcendental qualities of this ephemeral light source. Glass artists have long explored these aspects of the direct sun and its colorful components, from the rose windows of Gothic cathedrals to James Carpenter's dichroic glass installations like the window for the Christian Theological Seminary in Indianapolis, Indiana. These works may be as simple as the use of mirrors to scatter shards of light around an atrium or the delicate play of shadows across a wall or pavement.

The flexibility of electric light and its ability to be electronically controlled has inspired many interactive light/person installations. Laser light may be used to create lines or planes of light that bisect space and are only visible when they intersect a surface or person moving through the space. In his "solid light" series, artist Anthony McCall projected focused light downward into haze-filled rooms to create tentlike enclosures that were both sculpturally present and immaterial.[30] At times, McCall used digital animation to gradually morph the sculptured spaces into other forms. For the Interieur 2012 design event, artists from the Troika studio constructed a Gothic arcade solely from light, using focused "columns" of light and fresnel lenses to bend the light into the form of an arch.[31] Visitors to the exhibit walked down the Gothic passageway, running their hands through the columns of light.

The flexibility of LED sources has also spawned a range of light-responsive products that, at the largest scale, project mega images across the façade of a building or, at a smaller scale, may produce a swath of color as we move a hand across a wall or a foot across a light-paved surface. We touch the surface and it responds with light, either as an informational communication or as an artistic creation.

Light has the potential to set an overall tone for an entire geographic region or temporarily bring a smile to our face at the small sight of a shimmering rainbow of color. It has power in both its presence and its absence. Its intimate relationship with shadow shapes a yin/yang world with volumes of light and dark throughout everything we construct. An almost palpable manifestation, light space gathers us together in sunny alcoves or shadowed corners. It calls to our brightest hopes and our darkest fears, fills us with joy, places us in the spotlight or comforts us with soft anonymity. As designers, we are responsible for sculpting these places and bringing them to light (or darkness).

Notes

1   Steven Holl, "The Pantheon: A lesson on designing with light," Studio 360 [video], April 2, 2015, www.studio360.org/story/aha-moment-steven-holl-at-the-pantheon/
2   Fred Moody, "In praise of Seattle light," *The Weekly: Seattle's Newsmagazine*, January 21–27, 1987.
3   David Abram, *Becoming Animal: An Earthly Cosmology* (New York: Vintage Books, 2010), 15.
4   Ibid., 16.
5   Edward T. Hall, *The Hidden Dimension* (New York: Anchor Books, 1990), 42.
6   Ulrika Wänström Lindh, *Light Shapes Spaces: Experiences of Distribution of Light and Visual Spatial Boundaries* (PhD dissertation, HDK—School of Design and Crafts, University of Gothenburg, Sweden, 2012), https://gupea.ub.gu.se/handle/2077/31448), 22.

7   Juhani Pallasmaa, *The Eyes of the Skin: Architecture and the Senses* (West Sussex: John Wiley & Sons, 2005), 10, 13.

8   Lou Michel, *Light: The Shape of Space* (New York: Van Nostrand Reinhold, 1996), 62.

9   Wänström Lindh, *Light Shapes Spaces*, 22.

10 Christopher Alexander, Sara Ishikawa, and Murray Silverstein, with Max Jacobson, Ingrid Fiksdahl-King, and Shlomo Angel, *A Pattern Language: Towns-Buildings-Construction* (New York: Oxford University Press, 1977), 1160.

11 Gaston Bachelard, *The Poetics of Space* (Boston: Beacon Press, 1969), 170.

12 Richard Kelly, "Lighting as an integral part of architecture," *College of Art Journal* 12, no. 1 (Autumn 1952), 25.

13 Ibid.

14 Ibid.

15 Marietta S. Millet, *Light Revealing Architecture* (New York: Van Nostrand Reinhold, 1996), 51.

16 Alexander et al., *A Pattern Language*, 645.

17 Pallasmaa, *The Eyes of the Skin*, 47.

18 Jun'ichiro Tanizaki, *In Praise of Shadows* (Stony Creek: Leete's Island Books, 1997), 20.

19 Ralph L. Knowles, "The solar envelope," personal web page, 1999, www-bcf. usc.edu/~rknowles/sol_env/sol_env.html

20 Linnaea Tillett, email message to author, October 29, 2015.

21 See, for example: Millet, *Light Revealing Architecture*; Lou Michel, *Light: The Shape of Space* (New York: Van Nostrand Reinhold, 1996); Derek Phillips, *Daylighting: Natural Light in Architecture* (Oxford: Architectural Press, 2004); Gary Gordon, *Interior Lighting for Designers* (Hoboken: John Wiley & Sons, 2003).

22 NLPIP, "What is color rendering index?" *Lighting Answers* 8, Issue 1, Lighting Research Center, October 2004, www.lrc.rpi.edu/programs/nlpip/lightinganswers/lightsources/whatisColorRenderingIndex.asp

23 Timothy A. Schuler, "The evolution of white light," *Architectural Lighting*, August 12, 2015, www.archlighting.com/technology/the-evolution-of-white-light_o

24 C. Bushdid, M. O. Magnasco, L. B. Vosshall, and A. Keller, "Humans can discriminate more than one trillion olfactory stimuli," *Science* 343, no. 6177 (March 2014), 1370–2.

25 Lois Swirnoff, *Dimensional Color* (Boston: Birkhauser, 1988), 1.

26 Frank H. Mahnke, "Color in architecture – more than just decoration," *Archinect Features*, July 20, 2012, http://archinect.com/features/article/53292622/color-in-architecture-more-than-just-decoration

27 Ibid.

28 See for example: Daylighting Lab, *Building Daylighting Models* (Department of Architecture, University of Washington, Seattle), www.fau.usp.br/cursos/graduacao/arq_urbanismo/disciplinas/aut0213/Material_de_Apoio/Building_daylighting_models_tips.pdf (accessed July 20, 2016).

29 "MIT Infinite Corridor Astronomy – MIThenge," http://web.mit.edu/planning/www/mithenge.html (accessed July 20, 2016).

30 Stephen Johnstone and Graham Ellard, "Anthony McCall" *BOMB* 97, Fall 2006, http://bombmagazine.org/article/2841/anthony-mccall

31 Kortrijk, "Arcades by Troika," *Disegno*, October 29, 2012, www.disegnodaily.com/article/arcades-by-troika

Somatic Space

Chapter 4

"As we open a door, our body weight meets the
weight of the door; our legs measure the steps as
we ascend a stair, our hand strokes the handrail
and our entire body moves diagonally and
dramatically through space."[1]

Juhani Pallasmaa

"Why are emotions called *feelings*, and not *sightings* or *smellings*?"[2] Neuroscientist and bestselling author David Linden poses this intriguing question as he delves into the visceral connection between human touch and our emotional response to the world. We reveal our subconscious understanding of this link when we say that something "touches us," meaning that it affects us deeply. The somatic senses encompass this realm of touch and the body's knowledge of its own position and movement through space.

It has been argued that touch, the "lowest sense," is the oldest and most primal.[3] While vision distances us from the world, touch unites us with it. If something is close enough to touch you, it's also close enough to soothe and protect you … or to harm you. A startling research study in the late 1950s demonstrated that for an infant, tactile stimulation can be even more desirable than food. American psychologist Harry Harlow conducted an experiment with rhesus monkeys that had been raised without mothers. The infant monkeys were given a choice between two artificial surrogate mothers. Although both were constructed of rough wood and wire mesh, one was equipped with a bottle of nourishing milk while the other was covered with soft cloth. To the surprise of researchers, the monkeys consistently chose to spend time with the soft "mother" even though it had no source of nutrition.[4] Though the methods and conclusions of this research have been questioned, subsequent studies using subjects ranging from baby rodents to preemies in neonatal care units have reinforced the critical importance of tactile stimulation.

Even as adults, the sensation of touch exerts powerful influence over how we perceive things. In a study at Yale University, a research team asked participants to evaluate job candidates based only on a résumé. The results

Somatic Space

showed that if participants were handed the résumé on a heavy clipboard, they ranked the candidate as significantly more qualified than if they received exactly the same résumé on a lighter clipboard. The researchers postulated that this might reflect how we equate heavy with serious; thus, a heavy object may convey competence in much the same way a firm handshake does.[5] So it is a small step to ask of our built environment:

> "Does a heavy cold smooth door with a warm wooden handle have a different effect than a rough light warm door with a cold steel handle? … Does a door's weight influence our perceptions of a space as we enter it?"[6]

What exactly is the role of touch in our experience of place?

Our *somatic senses* encompass a range of different interactions, from the feel of a surface texture to more complex haptic and kinesthetic experiences. In the exploration of the built environment, we sometimes think of touch as being a more or less two-dimensional exploration with the hands. *Haptic* exploration extends this to a three-dimensional understanding of the form of objects and their spatial relationship to each other. Expanding further, kinesthesia describes the whole body's contact with and movement through the environment. At least one part of our body is touching the built environment all the time. The soles of our feet push against the floor; we grasp a door knob, close a cupboard, lean back against a wall, run our fingers along the wainscoting, ascend a stairway. In each of these actions, our body carries on a dialogue with our surroundings. Touch is a reciprocal sense—we touch something and it, in turn, touches us back. Moreover, touch is a sense that is always with us—we can't turn it off. We can close our eyes or cover our ears, but we can't stop feeling the world around us.

As infants, touch helps us calibrate visual information. We learn to combine visual and tactile sensory signals to comprehend the three-dimensional world around us. As designers shape and specify objects and surfaces in the built environment, they make a statement about care and thoughtfulness by the form and texture they create (Figure 4.1). The door handle shaped to the hand and rubbed smooth to the touch, the banister curved to the direction of movement, the seat molded to the form of the body—all of these are a direct tactile communication of care from the maker to the user. It says you are welcome here or you are not. It says that the maker has thought about you, has planned for this moment of your arrival, or that you are just one of many who pass through here and the building cannot be bothered to give attention to such a common and inconsequential event. It is a small, subtle greeting card that we all subconsciously read and remember. It is also a self-perpetuating process—a thing worn smooth with touch begs for more attention, more touching. The nose of the bronze door knob that is rubbed to smoothness by the ancestor's hands calls for the next generation to continue rubbing it to a golden luster. Its function of giving entry thus gives double pleasure—the pleasure of the touch and

Figure 4.1 An old brass door handle, polished to a golden luster by years of touch, lets us know this is a well-used building in a culture whose custom is to enter through the right-hand door.

the pleasure of the association with hands that touched it before.

But touch is a highly controversial sense. In its extremes, touch takes us to the highs of sexual pleasures and the lows of violent conflict and exposure to germs and disease. Touch requires closeness, intimacy. It limits the acquisition of information to the immediate area, within arm's length. So compared to sight, which conveys information at a safe, antiseptic distance, touch requires contact and has historically been considered "impure." This bias was reinforced as the germ theory of disease, first proposed in the sixteenth century, led us to understand the role of touch in the transmission of disease by microorganisms. Today, precautions around this dark side of touch abound, exemplified by the preponderance of bacterial wipes next to grocery carts at the local supermarket.

A SENSE OF THE BODY

Although touch is considered one of the five traditional senses, it's not located in a centralized sense organ like the other senses but is dispersed throughout the body. In medicine, the common term "touch" is usually replaced with "somatic senses" to better reflect the variety of mechanisms involved. These mechanisms include mechanoreception (touch), proprioception and kinesthesia (the understanding of our body extended in space and moving through it), thermoreception (temperature) and nociception (pain). The somatic system is most obvious in our skin, which is the body's largest organ, weighing from six to ten pounds.[7] But somatosensory receptors also reside in epithelial tissues (membrane tissue covering internal surfaces of the body), skeletal muscles, bones and joints, internal organs and the cardiovascular system. This complex sensory system involves a variety of receptors and processing centers that provide critical information about the state of our body and the world around it.

The built environment exhibits somatic qualities in many different ways and at many different scales. A tourist strolling across the Piata Mare square in Sibiu, Romania, registers the texture and form of the cobblestones under her feet while she dynamically feels the dimension of the square as the full motion of her body moves across it. If a light wind is blowing, she will sense the pressure of a cooling breeze fluttering against her bare arms. All of these represent a haptic connection between the environment and the occupant. This chapter explores the architectural experience of touch and also the experience of proprioception. The following chapter addresses temperature as a separate topic since, architecturally, the thermal environment is usually envisioned separately from the textural properties and is addressed by engineering specialists at a different part of the design process. The experience of nociception (pain) will only be alluded to as an extreme of the sensation of touch.

The physiology of our somatosensory system presents further complexities. When our hands probe the texture of a surface, we don't register a simple feeling of "touch." Instead, we experience an intricate combination of stimuli relating to pressure, skin stretch, vibration, temperature, etc. that are detected by a variety of specialized sensory receptors. Each neuron that transmits sensory information responds to stimulation of a very specific region of the skin (its "receptive field"). In body appendages like fingertips, these regions are quite small (2 to 3 mm), allowing us to differentiate fine textural details. The regions get considerably larger as they progress to the palm, lower arm, shoulder and back, which require greater variations in textural pattern for detection of this detail (up to 45 mm).[8] Because our body parts have these different sensitivities to touch, it is important to consider which body part will be in contact with each part of an object or structure in the built environment.

Once the touch stimulus has been activated, its sensory information travels inward toward the spinal cord and onward to the brain through specialized neurons which vary in size, structure and properties depending on the sensory information they convey. The part of our brain that processes most touch information, the somatosensory cortex, is like a highly distorted map of our body's surface. It overrepresents areas that have a high density of fine touch receptors (like the face, the lips, the tongue and the fingers) and underrepresents the low-density areas (like the small of our back, chest and thighs). The complexity of textures that we experience is not limited to the variety of sensors we have. As David Linden reminds us,

> "The real tactile world is wonderfully messy and complicated. … In the early part of the twentieth century, psychologists studying perception began to recognize that many of the most important and motivating tactile sensations, such as wetness, greasiness, or stickiness, might not be basic touch senses with dedicated detectors in the skin, but rather what they came to call touch blends."[9]

It's in the decoding of these touch blends that the brain works its magic, and like our other sensory systems, this is not a simple decoding process. Our touch circuits don't faithfully reproduce the outside world, but are arranged and linked to make inferences about that world based upon expectations from both the historical experience of our human ancestry and our own individual experiences.[10] Our touch responses are also not limited to direct contact with our body. We are able to project our haptic perception through tools that we use. For example, when we dig with a shovel, we can perceive tactile phenomena at the spoon end of the shovel almost as if our fingers were there. This "extended physiological proprioception" is accomplished by Pacinian touch sensors, which provide high-fidelity information of these stimuli to the hand by objects that it holds.[11]

Some haptic interactions with the world occur through no volition of our own, but arise when an outside force acts upon our bodies. This may happen when we turn a corner and a wind whips the air around us or when another being moves into contact with us. We are wired to pay more attention to these outside touches than those that result from our own movements. David Linden notes that

> "when we walk down the street, we barely notice the sensations of our clothing moving against our skin. However, if we experienced these identical sensations while we were standing still, they would be very conspicuous and would demand our immediate attention: Who or what is rubbing up against us?"[12]

The relative position of buildings and the openings in them shape this haptic space of moving air as they create protected wind shadows or intensified wind funnels that exaggerate the flow. The moving air that caresses our skin is continually feeding us information about the shape and proximity of the natural and built environment surrounding us. This is the touch of the world around us, and we, in turn, touch back.

TEXTURE

Touch puts our body in contact with architectural materials as they change in texture, form and density. In many buildings, we move from the roughness of the outside to the relative smooth of the inside. In others, roughness

Figure 4.2 This railing in the Starbucks Roastery and Tasting Room in Seattle is polished to a tantalizing sheen that begs to be stroked. Laser-engraved words provide microtexture that draws our touch and our attention.

follows us in to connect interior with exterior or to emphasize the rustic nature of the space within. Textures throughout a building invite us to engage with surfaces or shy away from them. We interact with this texture on many different levels, sometimes consciously exploring the finely carved flutes of a Grecian column, sometimes absent-mindedly stroking the edge of a countertop as we wait for a cappuccino (Figure 4.2).

Aidlin Darling Architects explored a full range of textures in their 2014 renovation of Skyhaus. Honoring the spirit of Joseph Esherick's original design, Aidlin Darling opened up the center of the house to a multistoried skylit garden atrium. This space, spanning Earth and sky, heavy and light, is united by a sculpted screen wall that reaches from the ground to the upper story (Figure 4.3). Filtering

Figure 4.3 The interior bridge of Aidlin Darlings's renovation of Skyhaus (top) contrasts a strongly textured porous screen wall on one side with glass and smooth finishes on the opposite. Viewed directly (bottom), the sculpted wall invokes the abstract shape of a tree (Aidlin Darling Design, San Francisco, 2014).

and animating light in the space, the wall also plays with texture at the micro, meso and macro levels. Micro-texture occurs at the level of the material and gives us information about what a substance is and how it has been created or finished. The Skyhaus screen wall is made of planks of reclaimed knotty pine that have been treated only with a light wash, not concealing the pine's natural irregularities. So at the micro scale, this screen has a directional grain with a slightly abrasive texture. Meso-texture occurs at the level of form and gives us information about how materials have been shaped and put together in the environment. An example of this is the screen's outward face that is carved into a relief with the abstract shape of a tree. Macro-texture occurs at the level of elements repeating or contrasted across a room, building façade or landscape. At Skyhaus, an interior bridge intersects the atrium at the second level. The contrast between the highly textural screen divider on one side this bridge and the pristine smoothness of glass on the opposite side creates a macro-textural asymmetry that enlivens this central atrium.

The textural environment constantly transmits subliminal messages. A change of texture may signal a transition from one place to another. It can set a subtle boundary to an intimate gathering place or direct the pattern of movement through an open area. It can entice people toward a wall or away from it. To the subtle observer, a change of texture in the paving of a plaza can serve as a haptic landmark, just as a tower can serve as a visual landmark.[13] Repeated variations in texture are experienced as pattern. Textural patterns allow us to break down larger areas into smaller units. They can help us gauge our progress along a path or relate a building façade to our bodily dimensions.

ROUGH AND SMOOTH

There is a naturalness to rough surfaces that frequently conveys a sense of the origins of the material and its weathering over time. This use of texture grounds an object or building in a geographic region and its traditional ways of building (Figures 4.4 and 4.5). Roughness may either shun touch or call for a more careful interaction to explore its peaks and cavities. Roughness also gives a sense of solidity/materiality and so is frequently used on lower floors of a building to give "weight" to a structure. Smooth surfaces, on the other hand, beg to be touched, to be stroked and explored. They draw your hand toward them and imply a sense of caring or value. If they shine, they may tell a history of repeated use or rubbing. Their flatness may convey a sense of lightness or immateriality.

The phrase "to go against the grain" means to struggle with the norms of a culture. It also informs both the way to work a piece of wood and the way to stroke it to receive the most pleasure. It's a phrase that puts us in bodily communication with the texture of surfaces around us. To fully get the feeling for the texture of something (fabric, pebbles, etc.), we have to move our hand along it; otherwise, the sensations fade quickly and become just pressure. So we are compelled to move our hands to explore textures, either *with* the grain to feel their smoothness, as happens when we glide our hand down a polished banister, or *against* the grain to probe the roughness, as when we lazily drag an outstretched hand across the ribs of a fluted column to create a rhythm of sensation. Thus, texture can create a directionality in the environment.

The experience of roughness or smoothness is heightened by contrast. Frank Lloyd Wright emphasized textural contrasts to enliven both the exterior and interior of the house he designed at Fallingwater (Pennsylvania,

Figures 4.4 and 4.5 Two top-lit circular chapels work with the texture of massive stone to reach two different conclusions. Temppeliaukio Church (top) carved out of solid rock is rugged and angular (Timo and Tuomo Suomalainen, Helsinki, 1969). Kamppi Chapel (bottom) cradles stones polished smooth by water (K2S Architects Ltd., Helsinki, 2012).

1936–8; Figure 4.6). Built in a rugged ravine, the house is cantilevered over a vibrant stream. To emulate the texture of the adjacent rock outcroppings, Wright used stone from the site to build up the major structural piers and laid the stones in a rustic and random pattern as though the rock from the site pierced vertically through the house itself. But the horizontal cantilevered balconies were cast in especially smooth, light-colored concrete to create the greatest possible contrast with the rough, dark vertical piers.[14]

The use and popularity of textured surfaces has evolved throughout architectural history depending on the culture and methods of production. Rough surfaces were historically associated with unskilled craftsmanship, whereas smooth, polished surfaces were associated with painstaking artistry. But the rise of industrialization allowed craftsman-like smoothness to be achieved in the factory at minimal cost. Capitalizing on this new opportunity, surface textures were largely suppressed by International Modernism (1920–60) in an effort to dematerialize architecture and accentuate volume rather than mass. By 1930, avant-garde architecture had virtually no tactile texture. As smoothness became common, it started to be equated with factory production and ultimately with cheap mass production. In response, roughness and irregularity became associated with handmade quality.[15] Paul Rudolf's Art and Architecture building at Yale University (1958–64) represented a deliberate and dramatic change as it reintroduced texture to the exterior façade.[16] Contemporary architecture continues to reframe the role of texture in the built environment. For example, in the Bruder Klaus Field Chapel (Figures 4.7 and 4.8), Peter Zumthor uses a ruggedly sensuous interior texture to create a space of solitude and contemplation.

Figure 4.6 At Fallingwater (Uniontown, PA, 1938), Frank Lloyd Wright celebrated textural differences by contrasting rugged vertical elements of local stone with smooth horizontal cantilevers of cast concrete.

Figures 4.7 and 4.8 The heavily textured, mystical interior (bottom) of Bruder Klaus Field Chapel (Peter Zumthor, Eifel, Germany, 2007) is masked by its smooth rectilinear exterior (top). The interior was created by burning away a wigwam made of 112 tree trunks that were encased within layers of concrete, leaving behind a blackened cavity of charred walls.

FORM

As materials are shaped into objects, they take on the larger texture of form. *The Handbook of Touch* explains that to perceive a three-dimensional object through touch, it is necessary to integrate information about the stimulus impinging on each finger and information about the location of the fingers in space (proprioceptive information).[17] Because objects may be much larger than the hand, the brain integrates this information over time and space so that the whole shape of an object can be understood as the hand moves to touch different parts of it sequentially.

As this process is extended to our participation in the built environment, we come to understand objects and structures in relation to the measure and form of our own bodies. In the tradition of Vitruvius and Leonardo da Vinci's *Vitruvian Man*, Le Corbusier developed the *Modulor* in an attempt to relate the built environment to the dimensions of the human body, acknowledging that we feel our way in the world through our bodies. Some material shapes and forms clearly hold the imprint of the human body as they reflect the processes that were used to create them. For example, historic cobblestone streets exhibit the natural semicircular sweep of the artisan's arm in the pattern of their surface (Figure 4.9). The repetition of this movement resulted in a series of scallops as the artisan moved forward to progress the paving down the street. Also, the weight and dimensions of standard building materials often reflect the capability of the "average" craftsperson. The size of a stone is sometimes referred to as a "one-man rock" or "two-man rock" based on the number of men it would take to muscle it into position.

It is through the imagined movement of our bodies that we experience texture at the macro scale of the assemblages of buildings and landscapes that surround

Figure 4.9 The scallops of this old cobbled street in France still show the swing of the artisan's arm, reminding us of the person who created it.

us. Tall buildings that step back from the street like the terraced walls of a rock canyon are experienced differently from buildings that rise as a vertical shaft from the adjacent sidewalk. We can imagine how we might climb out of the terraced canyon, but we have a bodily understanding that we would need a mechanical lift to transport us up the vertical shaft. The requirement for an elevator moves the person from the subject of his or her own action to the object of an operation, and this has important implications on people's sense of belonging to place and their strength and vitality within it.[18]

DYNAMIC: PROPRIOCEPTION

This dynamic encounter between our muscles and the world around us engages the kinesthetic and proprioceptive parts of our somatosensory system. These are energetically explored in the life of an active child. My house faces a small courtyard with a paved walkway composed of randomly alternating large and small paving bricks. My five-year-old neighbor Thomas frequently hops from one large paver to the next, avoiding all the small ones. One day I asked him what would happen if he missed and landed on a small one. He replied simply, "I'd lose." I confessed that I also sometimes play this game and he flashed me a conspiratorial smile.

Somatic Space

In our movements, we participate in a two-way communication with all the surfaces we contact and the ever-present tug of gravity. Our muscles communicate the effort of pulling our body weight up a flight of stairs or of pushing a heavy door out of our way. We flow with confident strides across an open plaza or erratically weave our way through a crowded corridor. We feel our muscles strain as we ascend, feel them ease as we move down. Our movement may bump down a flight of stairs with the rhythmic tat-tat-tat of the descent, or it may flow smoothly down the gentle angle of a ramp. Each of these creates a different connection between our bodies and the floor plane—a muscle communication. Dancers are experts at interacting with dynamic somatosensory space. Bloomer and Moore note how

> "Martha Graham, the doyenne of modern dance in this country, would regularly base a set of exercises on the haptic experience of space; her students were asked to hold, push, pull and touch pieces of space and places in space. … The dancer and the space animate one another as partners."[19]

This dynamic understanding of somatosensory space involves both the sense of the relative position of neighboring parts of the body in space (proprioception) and the strength of effort being employed in movement (kinesthesis). The information about the position and movement of body parts relative to each other is communicated by sensors in muscles, tendons and joints. To ground this understanding of movement to the outside world, the vestibular sense of the inner ear informs us about our body's orientation relative to gravity and lets us know if we are being moved through space by an outside force or being propelled by our own muscles.

THE FEELING OF UP AND DOWN

Our position in vertical space affects how we perceive it (Figure 4.10). We may perch above some spaces looking down on all that is below; or we may huddle in the bowels of a space that towers above us. Our body works to move from one to the other and we come to know the expanse in our body muscle memory. In *Body, Memory, and Architecture*, Bloomer and Moore describe the body's understanding of the single-family house with its "attic full of recollections of *up*, and a basement harboring implications of *down*."[20] They go on to say that "without the opportunity to ascend and descend, to enjoy the feelings of aspiring to heaven and the returning to earth, our journey may be a dispirited one."[21] And later they point out that

Figure 4.10 At the Kiasma Museum of Contemporary Art (Helsinki, 1998), Steven Holl links two forms, a rectilinear bar and an arching curve, and interweaves a circulation path between them. This moves visitors through an almost palpable space, along and through, above and below the architectural forms.

"movement upward can be interpreted as a metaphor of growth, longing, and reaching, and movement downward as one of absorption, submersion and compression."[22]

Le Corbusier's vertical circulation in Villa Savoye presents two very different experiences depending on the path taken. As the occupant ascends the stairway, the motion is clockwise, curvilinear and broken by the staccato rhythm of the steps. The alternate route, a two-segmented ramp, is counterclockwise, rectilinear and gradually sloped in its vertical progression. Movement along the two paths happens at right angles to each other, and they are arranged so that those moving along the paths brush past each other at only one point—the mid-level of the stair path and the full level of the ramp path. Each of these paths engages the body in a very different pace and rhythm of movement, accompanied by constantly changing views. Bloomer and Moore note how "it is most exhilarating when we can sense our movement in relation to a person on the other path, catching and losing sense of that person, playing curve off straight and step off stride."[23]

FROM HERE TO THERE

The first step of a movement implies a decision about which way to go. Some buildings take advantage of the push/pull of vertical space to impart a directionality to the progression. For example, the spiral circulation paths at the Guggenheim Museum (Frank Lloyd Wright) and the Seattle Central Library (Rem Koolhaus) encourage people to take the elevator to the top floor and then spiral down, rather than vice versa.

When we are faced with a choice about direction, the connection of somatic space with sight is important. We experience places differently if we can visually see the forward progression of the path the body is traveling so that we can take in the route in larger conceptual leaps and understand the choices available[24] (Figure 4.11). In this way, the path represents a concretization of progress or time.

In *The Poetics of Space*, Bachelard celebrates the common path, exclaiming: "And what a dynamic, handsome object is the path! How precise the familiar hill paths remain for our muscular consciousness!"[25] The presence of a path may be as simple as a change of texture in the ground plane, which may be continuous along the path or broken into segments as in a set of stepping stones. More elaborate textural paths may involve three-dimensional

Figure 4.11 A path foretells our forward movement. This path in Tanner Springs Park proposes a jagged course along the edge of a developed wetland. Reclaimed rail tracks form a strongly textured art wall along its eastern side (Atelier Dreiseitl and GreenWorks PC, Portland, 2005).

Somatic Space

engagement with the whole body. For people who are partially sighted or non-sighted, directional haptic cues are essential for supporting safe navigation through an environment. In the design of the Hazelwood School in Glasgow, Architect Alan Dunlop developed a haptically coded meandering plan that allows students (who are both blind and deaf) to independently navigate through the building. In addition, the interior walls are clad with multiple textured materials that pupils can follow with their hands to orient themselves within the school. This allows them to make their way from classroom to classroom with minimal help, increasing their confidence despite the challenges they face.[26]

LEAVING OUR MARK

Our somatic interactions also let us modify and manipulate the world around us. We cannot change our environment through hearing, seeing, smelling or tasting but we can through haptic body movements. A growing number of new materials celebrate this interaction by encouraging people to play with their environment through the sense of touch. The Miranda wall surface by the Giles Miller Studio in London consists of thousands of tiny plastic hairs that can be brushed in any direction to present an ever-adaptable surface appearance. Color-changing tiles responding to temperature (thermochromics) alter their hue when warmed by the human hand, while other modular surface materials light up when touched. The explosion in the use of touch screens suggests that they are ripe for development as future building materials. Google's development of touch-sensitive fabrics is now being explored for clothing, but these fabrics may also find their way into the built environment. The temptation to touch, and leave your mark, is impossible to resist.

HEAVEN AND EARTH

The dichotomies of somatic experience (up/down, light/ heavy, soft/hard, smooth/rough) call us to the ethereal reaches of heaven (up, light, soft, smooth) or ground us in the dense reality of Earth (down, heavy, hard, rough). They represent the most direct contact of our bodies with the material world around us and, thus, provide opportunities to craft textures and forms that call our hands to touch, our backs to relax against, or our bodies to dance and climb. As we have seen, they can move us along a path or stop us in our tracks. They push and pull our bodies as we move from one place to the next or stop to settle into the polished curve of a wooden bar stool. They whisper of the past, beacon to future possibilities, ground us in a place and add great depth to the here and now.

Notes

1 Juhani Pallasmaa, *The Eyes of the Skin: Architecture and the Senses* (West Sussex: John Wiley & Sons, 2005), 63.
2 David Linden, *Touch, The Science of Heart, Hand and Mind* (New York: Viking, the Penguin Group, 2015), 3.
3 Diane Ackerman, *A Natural History of the Senses* (London: Phoenix, a division of Orion Books Ltd., 2000), 80.
4 Harry F. Harlow, "The nature of love," *American Psychologist* 13 (1958), 673–85.
5 Elizabeth Gudrais, "The power of touch," *Harvard Magazine*, November–December, 2010, http://harvardmagazine.com/2010/11/the-power-of-touch (accessed July 20, 2016).
6 Christopher N. Henry, "Tactile architecture: does it matter?" *ArchDaily*, November 23, 2011, www.archdaily.com/186499/tactile-architecture-does-it-matter
7 Desmond John Tobin, "The anatomy and physiology of the skin," chapter 1 in *The Handbook of Touch: Neuroscience, Behavioral, and Health Perspectives*, ed. Matthew J. Hertenstein and Sandra J. Weiss (New York: Springer Publishing Company, 2011), 28.
8 Sliman J. Bensmaia and Jeffrey M. Yau, "The organization and function of somatosensory cortex," chapter 7 in *The Handbook of Touch: Neuroscience, Behavioral, and Health Perspectives*, ed. Matthew J. Hertenstein and Sandra J. Weiss (New York: Springer Publishing Company, 2011), 165–6.
9 Linden, *Touch, The Science of Heart, Hand and Mind*, 193.
10 Ibid., 196.
11 Ibid., 46.
12 Ibid., 197.
13 Jasmien Herssens, Ann Heylighen, and K. U. Leuven, "Haptic design research: a blind sense of place," *Proceedings of the ARCC/EAAE 2010 International*

Conference on Architectural Research, Washington, DC, June 23–26, 2010, www.aia.org/aiaucmp/groups/aia/documents/pdf/aiab087187.pdf

14 Leland M. Roth and Amanda C. Roth Clark, *Understanding Architecture: Its Elements, History, and Meaning* (Boulder: Westview Press, 2014), 85.

15 Ibid.

16 Ibid.

17 Bensmaia and Yau, "The organization and function of somatosensory cortex," 171.

18 Kent C. Bloomer and Charles W. Moore, *Body, Memory, and Architecture* (New Haven: Yale University Press, 1977), 62.

19 Ibid., 58.

20 Ibid., 1.

21 Ibid., 42.

22 Ibid., 59.

23 Ibid., 68.

24 Ibid., 88.

25 Gaston Bachelard, *The Poetics of Space* (Boston: Beacon Press, 1969), 11.

26 The Angry Architect, "The architecture of perception: 5 spaces designed to stimulate your senses," *Architizer*, February 25, 2015, http://architizer.com/blog/the-architecture-of-perception/

Thermal Space

Chapter 5

"Where vision has made architecture an object, heat will emphasize the links between objects, between objects and environment and between objects and time. The architecture of heat is about how life is lived within."[1]

Boon Lay Ong

The language of heat permeates the world of our attractions and repulsions. We divide people around us into those who are warm- or cold-hearted. We say an attractive person is "hot." We warm up to new ideas, get cold feet if something's too threatening and blow hot and cold if we're undecided. We distance with a cold stare, beckon with a warm smile, take time to cool down after heated arguments and lose ourselves in the fire of passion. Clearly, temperature is a hot topic for humanity.

In our built environment, also, the thermal realm is charged with strong emotions. Early in human history, warmth and the smell of food cooking—two critical life-sustaining elements—were connected to the central hearth. Fire also provided light in the night and protection from predators. Vitruvius went so far as to credit fire with the creation of human community:

> "The men of old were born like wild beasts, in woods, caves, and groves, and lived on savage fare. As time went on, the thickly crowded trees in a certain place, tossed by storms and winds, and rubbing their branches against one another, caught fire, and so the inhabitants of the place were put to flight, being terrified of the flames. After it subsided, they drew near, and observing that they were comfortable standing before a warm fire, they put logs on and while keeping it alive, brought other people to it, showing them by signs how much comfort they got from it. ... Therefore it was the discovery of fire that originally gave rise to the coming together of men, to the deliberative assembly, and to social intercourse."[2]

The warmth of the fire came to symbolize protection, community and life itself (Figure 5.1). The word "hearth," once just a descriptor for the floor of the fireplace, has become synonymous with family life and home. Hestia, the Greek goddess of the hearth, was the protector of

Figure 5.1 This inglenook in the House at Wind Point provides a cozy thermal alcove for family gathering. The words of Yeats' poem "The Lake Isle of Innisfree," inscribed on the walls, reinforce the sense of tranquility and connection with nature in this sustainable woodland refuge (Max Levy Architect, Lake Tawakomi, Texas, 2007).

I will arise and go now, and go to Innisfree,
And a small cabin build there, of clay and wattles made:
Nine bean rows will I have there, a hive for the honey bee,
And live alone in the bee-loud glade.

And I shall have some peace there, for peace
Dropping from the veils of the morning to
There midnight's all a glimmer, and noon
the linnet's wings

the home, family and state. In ancient Greece, each state or village possessed its own central hearth and sacred fire, kept alight continuously. The later Greek prytaneum contained this public fire which represented the unity and vitality of the community. Letting the fire go out was considered an omen of disaster.

Still today, we find this sense of community and camaraderie associated with warmth and a central fire. Marcel Proust poetically describes a fireside space as sensed by the skin: "a sort of alcove without walls, a cave of warmth dug out of the heart of the room itself, a zone of heat whose boundaries were constantly shifting and altering in temperature as gusts of air traversed them."[3] The Danish concept of *hygge* (often loosely translated as coziness) captures this sense of well-being through good times with close friends gathered around a fire with candles burning.

The central fire's corollary for the hot/arid climate is the courtyard or enclosed garden (Figure 5.2). This refuge from the heat is as central to Islamic or Hispanic culture as the hearth is to the home in cold northern cultures. In arid climates with clear skies, the shape of a courtyard traps cool night air. During hot daytimes, the shade of the tall walls, lush plantings and the evaporative cooling from fountains and plants maintains this coolness, creating a refreshing refuge.

Lisa Heschong's seminal book *Thermal Delight in Architecture*[4] awakens designers to the rich history of thermal experiences like these in our built environment. The book is a sensitive and insightful exploration into the design potential for thermal qualities and how they have manifested in a broad spectrum of cultures around the world. Through her investigations, we come to see how the necessity of coolness and warmth has become a symbol

Figure 5.2 In clear, arid climates, a courtyard provides a cool refuge, trapping chilly night air to temper daytime heat. Frequently, entry to the courtyard passes through a dark, covered area (the *zaguán*) that exaggerates the transition to the lush interior garden.

Thermal Space

not only of the family and community but also of the sacred.

Yet as houses evolved over the past century, the great central gathering fire was dispersed into smaller fires specialized for different functions—one providing warmth, a different one for cooking food and yet another providing light. Over time, many of these early fires were replaced with electric elements. And now, even the central hearth itself has disappeared or flattened to a two-dimensional image as central heating warms spaces to a comfortable 68°F (20°C) and digital fires blaze and crackle on video screens in living rooms. One promotional video promises "the element of visual and audio fire to heat you up" and informs us that to cool down, we can watch the "Redwood Creek Forest video with authentic on-location creek sounds."[5] There is both a touching nostalgia and an astute marketing observation in this phenomenon—a testimony to the fact that we are still animals, drawn to cooling water or a warming fire like a moth to light. Though they may entertain us for a while, how satisfactory are these two-dimensional visual facsimiles that we view from a distance and turn on or off with the flick of a switch? For it is our whole body, not our eyes alone, that longs for the cozy warmth of the fire or cool comfort of the forest stream.

IN SEARCH OF PARADISE

At the suggestion of David Linden,[6] I have typed the word "paradise" into an Internet image search engine. Sure enough, it returns tropical images of white sand beaches in the sunshine. As he points out, apparently paradise is a place where our bodies don't have to work very hard to maintain our core temperature. Although humans evolved in tropical climates with temperatures that supported life without additional heating or cooling, the discovery of fire allowed migrations to a wide range of climates that would kill a human without protective enclosures and heat sources. Thermal space is unique because it alone among the sensory spaces has the potential to be life-threatening if it fluctuates too far in one direction or the other. And it alone is commonly encountered outside the realm of ranges that support life. Death occurs if our core body temperature rises above 113°F (45°C) or drops below 77°F (25°C).[7] For warm-blooded animals like humans, regulating this interior temperature is a delicate balance between our bodies and the environment. Early buildings served the dual purpose of providing protection from predators and the discomfort of climate extremes. Whether as shade from the scorching sun or as an enclosure to hold in warmth, early buildings modified harsh exterior environments to improve comfort and safeguard life.

Our bodies are always generating heat from internal metabolism and muscular activity. Our core temperature is maintained by shedding heat to the environment when the body is overheated and taking on heat when it becomes cold. So sensing the thermal environment is a critical survival skill. We have different sensors in our skin for heat and cold, both tuned to our normal skin temperature, which hovers at around 91°F (33°C), somewhat below our core temperature. Lisa Heschong points out the unique characteristic of these sensors and the system they are part of:

"There is a basic difference … between our thermal sense and all of our other senses. When our thermal sensors tell us an object is cold, that object is already making us colder. If, on the other hand, I look at a red object it won't make me grow redder, nor will touching a bumpy object make me bumpy. Thermal information is never neutral; it always reflects what is directly happening to the body. This is because the thermal

nerve endings are heat-flow sensors, not temperature
sensors. They can't tell directly what the temperature
of something is; rather, they monitor how quickly our
bodies are losing or gaining heat."[8]

THERMAL BEIGE

Given the critical need for thermal regulation to maintain
life, it is not hard to understand how our buildings
evolved toward their current state of thermal uniformity.
The thermal environment was one of the first that our
modern world standardized. Instrumentation to measure
temperature is relatively simple and inexpensive, so it
has long been accessible to the building profession and
the lay public. This familiarity has made the language
of temperature commonplace. Most people can easily
tell you the temperature of an inside environment, but it
takes a specialist to tell you the decibels of sound or the
footcandles (lux) of light.

  In the United States, standardization of interior
temperatures was initiated by the American Society
of Heating and Ventilating Engineers (the precursor to
ASHRAE). This organization was first called to order in
1894 in New York City. Seventy-five engineers accepted
the invitation to the meeting (some of them from as far
away as the UK) and adopted a constitution that called for,
among other things, "a clearly defined minimum standard
of heating and ventilation for all classes of buildings."[9]
Through the following decades, these standards were
honed as more research money was spent on this aspect
of building services than in any other research field in
architecture.[10] Since comfort depends on how someone
is dressed, the engineers generated a numerical scale
for clothing (values ranging from 0.15 clo for a person in
underwear to 1.0 clo for a man in a lightweight business
suit to over 3.0 clo for insulated winter coat and hat)

and also quantified the description of progressive levels of activity (ranging from 0.9 MET for a sleeping person to 3.3 MET for a person walking to 10 MET for a person vigorously jumping rope). This all came together in the work of P. O. Fanger[11] who conducted research in the 1960s to develop a series of thermal comfort diagrams based on a seven-point scale of reported thermal comfort by male and female research subjects. His innovative work took into consideration all of the various heat exchange methods active in an environment to come up with a single formula to predict thermal comfort. This was compared against the predicted percentage dissatisfied (PPD) to anticipate the number of people who would complain about the thermal environment, with a goal of reducing complaints to below 20 percent (achieving comfort for 80 percent of the target population). As these early researchers worked toward this admirable goal of guaranteeing healthy interior environments for all, they also set the stage for boxing our world into a narrow range of acceptable temperatures, a veritable "thermal beige"[12] as it were.

For many years, Fanger's work formed the basis for the temperature thresholds in many countries, including the ASHRAE 55 Standard in the United States, and established the range of temperatures within which a building should fluctuate. But Fanger's work must be updated to fit the modern world. Although it has many nuances that address factors such as air speed and asymmetric distributions of radiant temperatures, it treats all occupants the same and assumes thermal comfort is a purely physiological equation. It doesn't take into account variables such as changing clothing norms, the increased percentage of women in the workforce, different cultural and geographical expectations, seasonal clothing and climate variations, and the amount of control that occupants have over their interior environment (whether from operable windows or from localized heating/cooling systems). Thus, it has led to women huddling under blankets in the modern workplace[13] and Bangladeshi offices being cooled to a Western ideal independent of local preferences.

Recognizing these deficiencies and intrigued by reports that people seem to prefer higher indoor temperatures in summer than they do in winter conditions, a number of researchers, including Gail Brager and Richard de Dear, started promoting an *adaptive* comfort model. This acknowledges that outdoor climate influences indoor comfort because humans adapt to different temperatures during different seasons.[14] It also acknowledges that other contextual factors, such as having access to operable windows and cultural thermal history, influence occupants' thermal preferences. This nuanced understanding of thermal preferences expands the temperature range accepted as being comfortable and opens the discussion of comfort to a wide range of factors outside of the physiologic and thermodynamic understandings of thermal exchange. Adding to the benefits of greater comfort, the adaptive strategy has the potential to save energy because it allows higher interior temperatures in summer (reducing cooling loads) and lower temperatures in winter (reducing heating loads). With this win-win situation, many current standards (including ASHRAE 55, ISO 7730 and the European Standard EN 15251) rushed to incorporate these new adaptive models.

COMFORT OR DELIGHT?

This new research guides us to a better understanding of thermal comfort, but is the goal of comfort enough? Is this rather like settling for a *sustainable* planet when you know that it can *thrive*? What about celebration, pleasure and delight? Heschong points out that "when thermal comfort is a constant condition, constant in both space and time, it becomes so abstract that it loses its potential to focus affection."[15] We need variation of the thermal environment across the space and the collaboration of our other senses to identify the source of our delight. We hold strong affinity for thermal anomalies in the environment, like campfires, tree-lined lanes, gazebos and even the oilcan fire on the street corner—these "thermal adiculae" as Heschong calls them. As this affinity is shared with others, these thermal spaces become beloved communal gathering spaces.

In fact, research shows that a static environment of thermal comfort precludes the opportunity for actual pleasure because when a person is in a state of thermal neutrality (comfort), any deviation from it will be perceived as unpleasant.[16] The only way to experience pleasure is to move from a state of discomfort to a state of comfort. This explains the rush of delight we experience when coming indoors on a snowy winter night or the titillation of placing one's body half in the shade, half in the sun on a brisk spring afternoon. In pursuit of thermal delight, the Finns run naked out of a scalding sauna to roll in the snow and sunbathers at a beach overheat in the sun before they plunge into the cold ocean.[17] Our uniform standards may provide us with comfort, but it seems that they also deprive us of the possibility for delight.

As uniform, standards-based environments spread internationally, we may also lose the delight of local customs and preferences. The southern porch swing and gazebo are often relegated to mere decorative elements in the landscape as air conditioning becomes more common and people retreat inside. Even the demise of the Mexican siesta can be attributed in part to the ubiquity of the air-conditioned office. An article in *The New York Times Magazine* noted that Mexican government workers took their last officially sanctioned siestas in 1999, heralding the passing of a cultural tradition and an important energy strategy. By shifting work from the hottest afternoon hours to the cooler evening hours, siestas provided de facto air conditioning for the office environment.[18] But now, the combination of air conditioning and global business practices has rendered the siesta obsolete. So although comfort is important, how do we expand our thinking about the thermal environment to reopen the possibilities of diversity and delight?

HUDDLES OF WARMTH; PUDDLES OF COOLTH

As we have seen, the contemporary engineering approach to shaping thermal space is to have the HVAC system fill the built space with a uniform temperature. We hold this thermal bubble within a tightly insulated envelope. Sometimes interior space is zoned so that some rooms are warmer or cooler than others. For example, the bedrooms may be kept cooler than the living room. But rarely do we intentionally exploit the full possibilities of creating thermal subspaces within a room or a garden or a neighborhood. Thermal nodes of warmth or "coolth" can be designed and shaped in our current architectural landscape just as four walls and a roof can shape a room. If we pay attention, we can sense their location, volume, intensity and boundaries.

CONDUCTION, CONVECTION, RADIATION, EVAPORATION

To design thermal spaces independent of architectural walls, it's important to understand how heat transfer mechanisms operate spatially. Our bodies have four ways to exchange heat with the environment: conduction, convection, radiation and evaporation.

Conduction is the transfer of heat that happens when our body touches a colder or warmer object and heat flows directly from the warmer object to the colder one.

When this happens, our body judges the coldness (heat flowing out of the body) or warmness (heat flowing into the body) by the rate of heat flow. So a material that conducts heat rapidly (a conductor) will feel colder or warmer than one that conducts heat more slowly (an insulator), even if they are at the same temperature. Thus, since wood is a relatively poor conductor of heat, on a cold winter day, a wooden bench outside will feel warmer than a steel one. But if the surface has been heated by the sun or mechanically heated above skin temperature, the opposite effect happens and the warmed steel bench or heated tile floor warms us more quickly than its wooden counterpart.

To warm a person with conduction, the person must be in direct contact with the warmed surface. This is the method used to efficiently warm passengers in electric cars with heated seats. But it may also be used architecturally. At Säynätsalo Town Hall in Finland, Aalto provided heating to the brick bench wall beneath the windows (Figure 5.3). This warms the layer of air in front of the windows to reduce their chilling effect on occupants and also creates a warm ledge for occupants to sit on adjacent to the window. This approach is also used in the warmed outdoor concrete benches at Amazon's Seattle Headquarters building. For conductive heating schemes like this, the area of impact matches the area of contact and the rate of heat flow is determined by the temperature and conductivity of the surface material.

Our bodies also lose or gain heat through *convective* heat exchange, which involves contact with materials that flow (fluids), such as air moving past our skin or water flowing around us, as a jump in a cold mountain stream will remind you. Even if the air is just a few degrees cooler than our skin temperature, significant cooling can happen as air currents continually siphon away body heat. This is one

Figure 5.3 In Säynätsalo Town Hall (Finland, 1952), Alvar Aalto used brick in the flooring and benches around the windows and then tucked heaters under the benches to provide conductive warmth in these window-side seats. Note also how the change of flooring materials delineates use.

reason why a cooling breeze or a porch swing provides such a refreshing relief on a hot afternoon (Figure 5.4). It also is the mechanism at work in the wind chill factor that can make winter weather feel much colder than the air temperature indicates.

Convective heat flows have two drivers: gravity and air currents. Hot air is lighter than cold air. In relatively calm conditions, gravity causes the lighter hot air to rise and cold air, which is denser, to collect at floor level. This natural stratification is why our feet may be cold even when the rest of our body is comfortable. Different cultures have evolved to take advantage of this stratification of heated air. For example, Europeans use chairs and beds to raise themselves conveniently above the cold air that accumulates at floor level, while many south Indians sit directly on the floor to benefit from the coolness there.[19]

Figure 5.4 A welcoming gazebo entices visitors in hot, humid climates. The covered top provides shelter from the sun's intense radiation while its open sides admit cooling breezes. Surrounding water or grassy areas help pre-cool air for increased comfort.

When an air current is present, the directional flow of the current overrides gravity to direct air movement. This pressure-driven convective air movement is the process at work in wind-driven ventilation cooling schemes and forced air heating and cooling systems. Simulation programs like computational fluid dynamics (CFD) can predict the patterns of hot and cold thermal regions in a building or landscape that result from these moving air streams.

Thermal energy can also travel directly through space from hotter objects to colder ones. Traveling almost 150 million kilometers (93 million miles) through empty space, the sun's rays warm the Earth's surface by this process of *radiation*. Collection of the sun's radiant energy is the basis of passive solar design strategies. But all other

Thermal Space

warm objects, including our bodies, also exchange heat by radiation with warmer and colder objects surrounding them. The radiation of heat between our body and a building surface depends on the temperature difference, the distance between them and the size of surface. If the surface is hotter than our skin temperature, it will radiate to our body; if the surface is colder, then it absorbs heat from us. Thus in a classroom, students sitting next to a large, very cold uninsulated window will lose more heat through radiation to the window and feel colder than students across the room. The cold surface of the single pane of glass draws heat from their bodies like a sponge. Insulated windows combat this heat drain with multiple layers of glass and low-e coatings that keep the inside pane of glass warmer, significantly reducing the chilly feeling.

Evaporation, the final heat transfer mechanism, cools our bodies by removing heat as moisture evaporates from our skin. The process of changing from a liquid to a gas requires a lot of energy (heat). As the skin's moisture evaporates, heat is absorbed and the adjacent skin is cooled. This is why our bodies have evolved to sweat in an attempt to lose heat by evaporative cooling when we're overheated. Evaporative cooling can also be used to cool building ventilation air in dry climates. For example, in hot, arid climates like that of the Middle East, traditional (vernacular) architecture sometimes incorporates a large wind tower (called a *malqaf*) that reaches up above building rooftops to catch the desert breezes (Figure 5.5). Frequently, this dry air is moved past moistened fabric or porous ceramic jugs of water so that water evaporates into the air, chilling it before it is directed down to occupied interior spaces. A similar process is used in modern-day evaporative coolers, but they have replaced the passive towers with motorized fans to generate air movement.

Figure 5.5 Vernacular cooltowers (*malqafs*) in Dubai were designed to catch high breezes and funnel them down into living areas. They frequently pass the incoming air across moistened fabrics or porous jugs of water to cool the air by evaporation.

All these mechanisms affect our experience of the surrounding thermal environment and are, thus, potential tools for designers to use to shape unique thermal places. Cultures around the world make different choices about whether to warm or cool a space through conduction, convection, radiation or evaporation or a combination of these mechanisms. For example, the conventional dining room in the United States is frequently warmed by convection as warmed air is circulated around the entire space. But in a passive solar house, the dining room may be heated by direct solar radiation that heats up a thermal mass in the room, such as a tile floor. This warmed mass then conducts and radiates heat to occupants. Alternately, in a traditional Japanese dining room, the air and surfaces

Figure 5.6 Traditional Japanese dining rooms are unheated, but diners are warmed by sitting around a heated dining table called a *kotatsu*. In this modern version, an electric heater under the table provides warmth and the quilt holds the warmed air near the occupant.

of the space may not be heated at all. Instead, diners sit around a heated dining table (called a *kotatsu*) covered with a thick quilt (Figure 5.6). Traditionally, hot coals were placed under the table, but today an electric heater is used. The quilt traps the heated air, thus warming the diners through both convection and conduction.

DIFFUSE AND ABRUPT BOUNDARIES

Insulated walls create abrupt thermal boundaries that can produce dramatic differences in temperature from outside to inside. Although thermal volumes that are not enclosed by solid walls frequently have gradual, diffuse boundaries, like the gradual dissolution of heat as one moves away from a campfire, this is not always the case (Figure 5.7).

Figure 5.7 People gathered in the shadow of the Torre del Mangia on the Piazza del Campo in Siena attest to the abrupt boundaries and refreshing allure of this cool thermal space on a hot sunny day.

Thermal Space

Thermal boundaries can be abrupt when conduction is the mechanism of heat transfer, as when a heated stone bench provides thermal comfort just to the people in direct contact with it or when a heated or chilled "air curtain" provides an invisible thermal boundary at an opening in a store façade. Shadows also provide abrupt changes in thermal zones when they block solar radiation to create a cooler space in the midst of a sunny landscape.

EARTH, WIND AND SUN

The chapter on light space noted how the Earth's movement around the sun and around its own axis orchestrates a sensory rhythm to the cycle of a day or a year. In summer when the planet leans toward the sun, the sun rises early, sets late and traces a high arc through the sky. In winter when the planet tilts back from the sun, solar angles are lower and the hours from sunrise to sunset are reduced.

This annual cycle is exaggerated as we move from the equator to higher latitudes. At the equator, the sun stays high overhead throughout the year and only lazily oscillates from south to north in the sky, changing the direction of the light but creating little difference in temperature. Moving toward the polar regions from either the tropic of Cancer or the tropic of Capricorn starts a cyclical variation of seasons, which intensifies as we approach the poles. As summer progresses to winter in these regions, solar rays travel longer through the Earth's atmosphere, so more heat is absorbed, their warmth is diminished and we experience the cold thermal extremes of freezing temperatures. These solar changes also drive regional wind and precipitation patterns, which combine to create the climatic personality of places around the world.

The solar energy hitting the Earth's surface every year is about 1,400 times more than our total energy needs.

Clearly, there is potential for us to create cozy gathering places powered by the warmth of the sun alone. Lisa Heschong describes the varied thermal environments that result from the simple act of placing a hut in the landscape:

> "As soon as a simple square hut is built, at least six new microclimates are created: the south side warmed by a sunny wall, the north side in shade most of the time, an east side with its morning sun and perhaps protected from the prevailing breeze and a west side warmed in the afternoon but buffeted by the wind. There is also the inside with its shelter from the rain and wind and sun, and the roof raised above ground level, more exposed to wind and sun."[20]

As we embody the knowledge of this sun and shade, we start to envision the magical thermal spaces that can evolve as they guide our designs. Some of them may be quite simple. In *A Pattern Language*, Christopher Alexander et al. urge that "the area immediately outside the building, to the south—that angle between its walls and the earth where the sun falls—must be developed and made into a place which lets people bask in it."[21]

The relatively steady temperature of earth can also shape a thermal cave of comfort in regions with a temperate climate. Due to the higher heat capacity of soil relative to air and the thermal insulation provided by vegetation, seasonal changes in soil temperature deep in the ground are much less than those of the air above. Thus in spring, the soil warms more slowly than the air, and by summer, spaces protected by layers of earth provide a cool refuge. Likewise in autumn, the soil releases its heat more slowly than the air, and by winter, it is warmer than the overlying air. So a space nestled into the earth or the side of a hill may provide a cool alcove in summer and temper a winter chill.

Figure 5.8 In the late 1190s, Ancestral Puebloans built stone dwellings beneath the cliff at Mesa Verde. The overhanging ledge shaded high-angle summer sun but invited lower-angle winter sun to warm the walls and interior spaces, thus modulating the thermal environment as needed for this hot summer/cold winter climate.

Vernacular architects (using the traditional building practice of a region) worked with the embodied knowledge of these daily and seasonal solar fluctuations and the thermal properties (absorption, transmission, reflection and emission) of building materials to create refuges appropriate to the local climate (Figure 5.8). The Mesa Verde cliff dwellings, for example, not only openly embrace the low angle of the winter sun for heating but also huddle into the hill and the shadow of the overhanging cliff for the cooling that is needed during hot summer months. These responses to the predictable movement of the sun through the sky at different latitudes and times of the day and year provide a poetic connection of buildings to the places we inhabit. Many characteristic regional building designs were driven by just this desire to create pockets of warmth or cool that gathered people at different times of day—the shaded verandah or gazebo of the hot/humid south, the courtyard in hot/arid climates, the thick bermed walls and cheery sunrooms of more northern climates. All of these create thermal niches that hold memories of camaraderie as well as a thermal relief from the climate's intensities.

There are many books available today that explore these passive and vernacular approaches to creating thermal comfort in the diverse climates around the world. They both elucidate the techniques of early builders and provide contemporary examples of buildings that create delightful thermal spaces using passive design strategies. For a more thorough review of these passive techniques, the reader is encouraged to take advantage of these resources.[22] We look to these examples not to copy the exact forms, as they arose in earlier times with different cultures and needs, but rather to appreciate their sensitivity to the natural flows and accumulations of heat and to learn to use these to sculpt thermal places in our future designs.

A LITTLE HELP FROM THE ENGINEERS

Today, we often rely upon mechanical systems to create thermal comfort. Contemporary engineering ingenuity enlists all the available heat exchange mechanisms (radiation, convection, conduction and evaporation) to condition thermal environments. Although by default they are often manipulated to produce a thermally uniform space that coincides with the tectonic shape of a building or a room, as with natural mechanisms, they may be

Figure 5.9 The radiant floor at the Desert Living Center in Las Vegas incorporates a see-through floor panel and a graphic depiction of the radiant dissipation of heat, showing how heat hovers in a layer above the floor at the level of the occupants (Lucchesi Galati Architects, 2007).

enlisted to shape a more interesting and energy-efficient thermal sensescape (Figure 5.9). For example, radiantly heated floors work with the natural principle of how heat rises to create a volume of warmth that hovers near the floor where the occupants are. This also saves energy because it doesn't waste heat at the unoccupied ceiling level. Similarly, radiantly chilled beams placed just above head height work with the natural convective tendency for chilled air to drop to cool the space at the occupant level. Localized radiant heaters can also be used to provide tightly controlled areas of warmth, and these are often used above a cluster of tables on a café patio to create a welcoming tent of warmth on a chilly evening.

Some of the best examples use a combination of natural and mechanical systems to sculpt thermal spaces that let people choose the thermal environment they want. The visitor center at Zion National Park, a canyon desert region of southwest Utah, is one of these (Figures 5.10–5.12). Its design starts with a passive solar approach and then layers engineered mechanical systems on top of the passive strategies to fine-tune the thermal spaces. Because visitors arrive in clothing suited to the outdoor temperature, temperatures inside the center are allowed to fluctuate

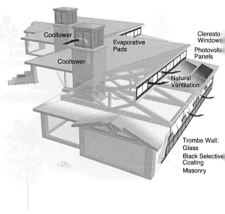

Cooltower

Evaporative Pads

Cooltower

Clerestory Windows

Photovoltaic Panels

Natural Ventilation

Trombe Wall:
Glass
Black Selective Coating
Masonry

Figures 5.10–5.12 The base of the cooltower at Zion National Park Visitor Center is a refreshing gathering place for tourists on hot summer days. Use of other passive design elements like daylighting, a trombe wall and direct solar gains in winter provide base comfort in the space. Radiant heaters boost warmth near staff areas as needed during cold months (National Park Service and Denver Service Center, 2000).

cooler in the winter and warmer in the summer. During the prime summer visitor season at Zion, the hot, dry desert climate often exceeds 100°F (38°C). But humidity is low and summer nights can be pleasantly cool or even chilly, dipping into the low 60s. During these hot summers, the cooling strategy involves two "cooltowers." These are oversized chimneys that collect warm summer air above roof level and passively chill it by evaporation of water from cooling pads suspended in the opening (similar to the Middle Eastern *malqaf*). This chilled air drops through the chimney and flows out of the opening at the bottom, creating a cool place (as opposed to a fireplace) where visitors gather to cool off and swap stories about the sculpted sandstone canyons and blistering heat. Small fans help to circulate this cool air to adjacent offices while hot air from the space is vented out through high, south-facing clerestory windows.

Winter temperatures, on the other hand, are frequently below freezing, so at this time of the year, the building closes inward, reducing its porosity. Openings in the cooltowers are shuttered and solar gains are collected. On the south façade, a trombe wall, consisting of a glazed surface in front of a thermally massive concrete block wall, soaks up solar gains in the daytime sun and reradiates this heat to the interior. High, south-facing clerestory windows also provide solar gains to warm the massive concrete floor. These both create an ambient level of comfort for jacket-wearing visitors. In addition, electric radiant heaters are positioned to produce small zones of warmth at locations where staff spend the most time, allowing for an overall lower thermostat set point in winter. This use of natural thermal resources and the shaping of thermal space in the visitor center helps it save over 60 percent of its energy use compared to a commensurate building with conventional heating, cooling and lighting systems.[23]

CHARTING THE THERMAL SENSESCAPE

As we have seen, we respond to a wide range of stimuli that shape the thermal sensescape around us. Our bodies explore these thermal sensations and probe their invisible boundaries and pleasures. Juhani Pallasmaa poetically reminds us that "the skin traces spaces of temperature with unerring precision; the cool and invigorating shadow under a tree or the caressing sphere of warmth in a spot of sun."[24] But as designers, we can also benefit from tools that anticipate the shape of these spaces before they are built. Unfortunately, since there is a wide range of factors affecting our thermal experience, there is no one tool that combines all of them. Many building energy simulation programs compute the temperature of building surfaces and uniform thermal zones and may provide information about static air temperatures within the building. For moving air, a CFD simulation is needed to predict the location and movement of thermal airstreams inside and outside buildings. Comfort software provides a third level of information about the average person's response to a set of thermal conditions, but this can't anticipate personal and cultural preferences and the anomalies of thermal delights that we have seen in this chapter.

So although these tools can provide useful information about the physical distribution of thermal conditions in a design, they are not a substitute for the actual experience of immersion in a sensory world. As Pallasmaa reminds us,

"basic architectural experiences have a verb form rather than being nouns. Authentic architectural experiences consist then ... of occupying the sphere of warmth, rather than the fireplace as an object of visual design. Architectural space is lived space rather than physical space, and lived space always transcends geometry and measurability."[25]

THERMAL SYNESTHESIA

Thermal pleasure or displeasure is also affected by more subtle physiological and psychological factors. So far, we have explored the thermal properties that affect core body temperature over time. But thermal comfort researchers Thomas Parkinson and Richard de Dear describe another mechanism that impacts our sense of well-being. They point out that a person can experience simple thermal pleasure even if only a small part of their body is warmed or cooled. For example, when we are cold, we commonly derive simple pleasure from wrapping our hands around a warm mug; or when we feel too hot, we enjoy a cold damp towel on our forehead.[26] These localized pleasure sensations are called spatial alliesthesia, a perceptual process driven predominantly by signals from the skin and different from the whole-body model driven from thermal impacts on the central core. As designers, we must consider both of these as our designs sculpt huddles of warmth and puddles of coolth in the landscape around us.

We may even experience warmth at times when there is no measurable thermal change to the environment. Unlike our eyes and ears, our thermal sensors aren't distance receptors. As Lisa Heschong reminds us,

"they cannot warn us that a place will be cold before it starts to chill our body, we have to rely on other senses to give us advance clues. We look for qualities that have been associated with warmth or coolness in our past experience. Does the place have soft fuzzy surfaces? Perhaps it will be warm like my wool sweater is. Are the colors reds and browns? Then maybe it will be warm like a room lit by the red-gold light of a fire. Are

Figure 5.13 The sauna is a center of both renewal and gathering in Estonian culture. The amber glow of wood for this one at the MEKTORY Innovation Center hints at the warmth that lies within, enticing visitors in from the relative cool of the adjacent blue-tiled bath area.

Thermal Space

there mellow aromas? Then surely it will be warm like a kitchen full of people and spices and bread baking. … Such clues from other senses can become so strongly associated with a sense of coolness or warmth that they can occasionally substitute for the thermal experience itself."[27] (See Figure 5.13)

This is thermal synesthesia—the substitution of one sense experience for another. It sometimes reinforces the sensory experience and, at other times, provides us mixed messages about what to expect. Hence, it may lead to the initial appeal of a video fireplace but end in disappointment as we find the sensory warmth missing.

THE HEART OF THE MATTER

As we have seen, the means of shaping a thermal alcove may be as simple as placing a window seat in the sunshine or digging a cave into the earth, or it may be more complex, involving technically sophisticated mechanical systems. In either case, what is important is that our bodies feel out these places of warmth or coolness and experience delight in them. These thermal spaces have the ability to ground us in a sense of home, a sense of safety and belonging— both to a place and to a community. They speak to us of the earthly rhythm of seasons and of the human rhythm of connection. In connecting us with place and the local climate, they also point the way toward a sustainable approach to inhabiting a planet with limited resources. When we flatten this experience to a monochrome of acceptable temperatures, we not only waste energy but also lose this poetic connection to hearth and home.

Notes

1   Boon Lay Ong, "Warming up to heat," *Senses & Society* 7, no. 1 (2012), 17.
2   Marcus Vitruvius Pollio as quoted in Lisa Heschong, *Thermal Delight in Architecture* (Cambridge: The MIT Press, 1982), 11–12.
3   Marcel Proust, *Remembrance of Things Past, Vol. 1*, Trans. C. K. Scott Moncrieff and Terence Kilmartin (New York: Vintage Books, 1982), 8.

4   Lisa Heschong, *Thermal Delight in Architecture* (Cambridge: The MIT Press, 1982).
5   "Fire trance—digital fire—a twist on the fireplace," *YouTube*, uploaded November 28, 2011 [video], www.youtube.com/watch?v=6FTzjR6WYf8
6   David Linden, *Touch, The Science of Heart, Hand and Mind* (New York: Viking, the Penguin Group, 2015), 139.
7   Boon Lay Ong, "Warming up to heat," 12.
8   Heschong, *Thermal Delight in Architecture*, 18–19.
9   "History of ASHRAE," *ASHRAE*, https://www.ashrae.org/about-ashrae/ashrae-and-industry-history (accessed July 20, 2016).
10   Reyner Banham, *The Architecture of the Well-tempered Environment* (Chicago: The University of Chicago Press, 1969), 40.
11   P. O. Fanger, "Assessment of man's thermal comfort in practice," *British Journal of Industrial Medicine* 30 (1973), 313–24, www.ncbi.nlm.nih.gov/pmc/articles/PMC1069471/pdf/brjindmed00096-0001.pdf (accessed July 20, 2016).
12   Term attributed to Professor Scott Wing at Penn State College of Arts and Architecture.
13   Pam Belluck, "Chilly at work? Office formula was designed for men," *The New York Times*, August 3, 2015, www.nytimes.com/2015/08/04/science/chilly-at-work-a-decades-old-formula-may-be-to-blame.html
14   Richard de Dear and Gail Schiller Brager, "Developing an adaptive model of thermal comfort and preference," *ASHRAE Transactions* 104, no. 1 (1998), 145–67.
15   Heschong, *Thermal Delight in Architecture*, 36.
16   Thomas Parkinson and Richard de Dear, "Thermal pleasure in built environments: physiology of alliesthesia," *Building Research and Information*, 43, no. 3 (2015), 289.
17   Heschong, *Thermal Delight in Architecture*, 21.
18   Maggie Koerth-Baker, "What does it mean to be comfortable?" *The New York Times Magazine*, January 25, 2013, www.nytimes.com/2013/01/27/magazine/what-does-it-mean-to-be-comfortable.html
19   Heschong, *Thermal Delight in Architecture*, 31.
20   Ibid., 8.
21   Christopher Alexander, Sara Ishikawa, and Murray Silverstein, with Max Jacobson, Ingrid Fiksdahl-King and Shlomo Angel, *A Pattern Language: Towns-Buildings-Construction* (New York: Oxford University Press, 1977), 758.
22   See, for example, David Bainbridge and Ken Haggard, *Passive Solar Architecture: Heating, Cooling, Ventilation, Daylighting and More Using Natural Flows* (Vermont: Chelsea Green Publishing, 2011); Mark DeKay and G. Z. Brown, *Sun, Wind, and Light: Architectural Design Strategies*, 3rd Edition (New Jersey: John Wiley & Sons, 2014); Donald Watson and Kenneth Labs, *Climatic Building Design: Energy-Efficient Building Principles and Practices* (New York: Mcgraw-Hill, 1993); Victor Olgyay, *Design with Climate: Bioclimatic Approach to Architectural Regionalism* (New Jersey, Princeton University Press, 2015).
23   P. Torcellini, N. Long, S. Pless, and R. Judkoff, *Evaluation of the Low-Energy Design and Energy Performance of the Zion National Park Visitors Center*, NREL/TP-550-34607, (Colorado: National Renewable Energy Laboratory, February 2005), 57–61.
24   Juhani Pallasmaa, "An architecture of the seven senses," in *Questions of Perception*, ed. Steven Holl, Juhani Pallasmaa, and Alberto Pérez-Gómez (San Francisco: William Stout Publishers), 33.
25   Ibid.
26   Parkinson and de Dear, "Thermal Pleasure in Built Environments," 292.
27   Heschong, *Thermal Delight in Architecture*, 23.

Acoustic Space

Chapter 6

"Anyone who has become entranced by the sound of dripping water in the darkness of a ruin can attest to the extraordinary capacity of the ear to carve a volume into the void of darkness. The space traced by the ear in the darkness becomes a cavity sculpted directly in the interior of the mind."[1]

Juhani Pallasmaa

The staccato clack-clacking of wood on wood bounces from one house to the next, echoes off the stone cliff across the valley and pummels me from all directions as I walk out of the village. This is the chorus of weavers whose farms trail a mile or two down the road away from town. Large wooden looms feature prominently on front porches of the houses that line the street. Morning is weaving time, before the heat of the day sets in. This rhythmic chatter of looms forms a background sound to the morning, commencing shortly after the first rooster crows, dying down as the sun hits the high point of its travel through the sky. This is the sound of Todos Santos Cuchumatán, Guatemala. It's the fabric of connection among the weaving households of the village, uniting them in a common task every morning, a lively chatter of camaraderie for solitary work. The sound hugs the valley, trailing off from town like a low lying cloud, and surrounds all that happens in that neighborhood—people tending fields of corn, teaching at the school, selling oranges beside the road. All work to the rhythm of the weaving. As a tourist, here to learn Spanish for a month at a local language school, I wander through the sound. I climb the hill above it and feel it fade to a faint chatter of crickets. I am a visitor to this sound. This is not my hometown drone of planes from Boeing Field or cars on a freeway. It is the sound of the making of a fabric that binds these people to each other and to their history.

Sound animates the world; it both surrounds us and emanates from us. As we hear and feel sound vibrations, we enter into an active relationship between our bodies and the beings and objects around us. Like the unique sounds of the weaving villages of Guatemala, each place on Earth has its voice (Figure 6.1). Acoustic ecology researcher R. Murray Schafer coined the term

Figure 6.1 An installation at a Seattle theater asked people to post sounds they heard near their homes on bulletin boards labeled "Where I Come From, You Can Hear the Sounds Of ... ." Comments captured sounds of the US coastal northwest including *foghorns and ferry boats, crickets, trucks and honking, the train behind our house, seagulls, thunderstorms, my mom teaching piano lessons.*

"soundscape" in the 1970s to describe the total sonic environment.[2] A number of different projects are working to capture these place voices. Victoria Meyers at the University of Cincinnati School of Architecture and Interior Design has her students record site sounds and make "sound sections" of existing neighborhoods in Cincinnati.[3] Taking the next step, several universities have set up websites to encourage people all over the world to record and upload sound clips of the unique sounds they encounter in their daily lives.[4] These "aural postcards" give us a snapshot of the acoustic environment, but they can't immerse us in the full acoustic experience. Like their picture postcard equivalents, there's no comparison to actually being there.

The soundscape is a complex space, confounded by the multiple levels of information we extract from it—the tone of a single musical note or syllable, the rhythm of a series of tones put together in a sequence through time, the recognition of symbolic meaning in a word or series of words in a sentence. We also receive spatial information from the initial direction of the sound and the reflections and echoes that give fullness to the sounds we hear. We are familiar with how sound lets us communicate ideas and information through language and how we experience sound aesthetically in music. But we think less about the role sound plays in providing information about our surroundings. This latter affect is often below our consciousness, but it is vitally important for the experience of our place in the world. As architect and sound artist Shea Trahan reminds us, "as a designer, we create architectural spaces which are de facto instruments—they contain sound, they manipulate it, they can even create sound—so we're tasked with a very powerful tool for affecting human cognition."[5]

In line with the emphasis on language and music, most research into architectural sound has been narrowly focused on three major areas of physical acoustics: the optimization of acoustics for the projection and enjoyment of music in performance halls; the reduction of reflected sound energy in spaces (classrooms, offices, etc.) where speech clarity is required; and the reduction of unwanted sound transfer (noise abatement) in a wide range of other spaces. These topics are extensively covered in other books,[6] so this chapter just touches on them briefly. Our focus here is on how we experience the sound space around us—the more subtle "aural architecture" of enveloping sound that provides information about the shape and materiality of our environment. Thus, although the study of physical acoustics and aural architecture are directly related, their emphasis is different. We can use the research on physical acoustics to help us understand the scientific laws involving propagation of sound waves in space, but to understand aural architecture, we must immerse ourselves in the experience itself.

Michael Kimmelman, architecture critic for *The New York Times*, brings the concept of aural architecture to life as he points out that

"Sound may be invisible or only unconsciously perceived, but that doesn't make it any less an architectural material than wood, glass, concrete, stone or light. … You don't need to be a specialist to distinguish spaces according to the sounds they make.

You can probably conjure the lofty, uplifting sound inside a great stone cathedral, like St. Patrick's in New York, just by thinking about it.

A bistro, like Lafayette in Manhattan, has a distinctive sonic profile that's textured, enveloping, open, bright. You can imagine the clink of glasses and plates, the scrunch of bodies on leather banquettes, the hum of voices reflecting off mirrors and windows. The sound is inextricable from the experience, like the smell of roast chicken or freshly baked bread. It's almost tactile.

[…]

While it's sometimes hard to pin down exactly how, there is often a correlation between the function of a place or an object and the sound we expect it to make. So an expensive, solid wood door sounds better than an inexpensive hollow one, partly because its heavy clunk reassures us that the door is a true barrier, corresponding to the task it serves.

[...]

If only subliminally, we also know, by contrast, when sound spoils architecture because it fails to correspond to function. The bygone Shea Stadium in Queens was joyless partly because the design of its low, wide semicircle dissipated the sound of a cheering crowd into Flushing Bay. Fenway Park in Boston is the reverse; it concentrates hometown joy."[7]

The online version of this article, complete with embedded video and three-dimensional audio, brings the added depth of the sonic environment to the reader.

In their seminal book *Spaces Speak, Are You Listening?*, Barry Blesser and Linda-Ruth Salter liken the impact of sound in exploring soundspace to the use of light in architectural design. They point out that "just as light sources are required to illuminate visual architecture, so sound sources (sonic events) are required to 'illuminate' aural architecture."[8] Although our ears and body feel out the lay of the soundscape similar to how our eyes probe the landscape, sound is different and, in some ways, more complex than light. A black curtain stops light but may allow sound to penetrate almost unaltered. Insulated windows, on the other hand, provide clear access to light and views but are effective barriers to sound. The temporal aspects of light and sound are also different. Turn off a light source and the space goes immediately dark; yet turn off a sound source and the space continues to speak. Perhaps the most interesting difference for the designer is that whereas the architect sees light space as his or her creation, the occupants have a major influence on the experience of its aural architecture. No single designer owns the aural architecture because without events in the space, there is no sound.[9]

SOUND/SILENCE/TIME

Our experience of sound has three primary features: the sounds we hear, the silence that separates them and the time duration of each. Sounds are further differentiated by their tone or pitch, their intensity and the dynamics of their mixing with other tones and reflections. The time duration is animated by its rhythmic pattern. The combination of all these yields the rich variety of sounds we encounter.

Observations on the physical phenomenon of sound date at least as far back as Aristotle (350 BC), who observed that sound results from the impact of two solids against each other and that when straw is strewn across the floor of an orchestra, background noise is reduced. But it wasn't until 1887 that John Rayleigh verified that sound is actually a radiating wave.[10] However, unlike light, which is an electromagnetic wave, sound is a mechanical wave made up of moving particles. Thus, although light can travel through a vacuum, sound requires a medium (solid, liquid or gas) to transmit it, similar to a wave on the ocean that moves through the water. In its essence, sound is a vibration, an alternating variation of compressions and expansions (rarefactions) of air pressure, emanating from a vibrating source and received by a listener. Ideally, sound propagates outward from the source in an expanding spherical shape. It moves from air molecule to air molecule until it encounters an obstacle, at which point it is absorbed into the surface or bounces back on itself, providing information about the shape, size and materials of the space it moves within. Thus sound represents a spatial event, a material phenomenon and an auditory experience all combined into one.[11]

Sounds are characterized by their wavelength, the time from peak to peak, which is inversely related to their frequency, the number of cycles per second or hertz (Hz).

Humans can hear sound in frequencies from 20 Hz to 20,000 Hz. The lower frequencies are low bass sounds, and the higher frequencies are high-pitched treble sounds. Below 20 Hz, we can detect body vibrations. Our ability to hear sound varies with its frequency. Our hearing is most sensitive at around 4,000 Hz and diminishes as frequencies get higher or lower. It is especially poor at the very low end of our frequency range, so we need higher intensity in the bass range to equal our experience of loudness in the mid-range or treble frequencies. However, in spite of our diminished sensitivity to them, low-frequency sounds have an important impact on the built environment because they pass more easily through solid barriers like glass windows and walls.

The speed of a sound wave is directly proportional to the density of the matter it travels through. For example, the speed of sound in air at room temperature is about 343 m/s, while in water, it is about 1,484 m/s, and in aluminum, 6,400 m/s.[12] We can calculate the wavelength of sound by dividing its speed by its frequency. Doing this, we find that sound waves are really quite large, at roughly the same scale as furniture and architectural elements. For example, the lowest sound we can hear has a wavelength about the length of a small banquet hall, while the highest tone has a wavelength about the width of your finger.[13]

Although many animals have more acute hearing than humans, we still have a wide range of sound intensities we can distinguish. But, as with some of the other senses, our reaction to intensity is not linear. That is, we don't experience the sound of ten people clapping as ten times the sound of one person clapping. Instead, it sounds only about twice as loud as one person. So the accepted scale for reporting the loudness (intensity) of sound is logarithmic and is reported in decibels (dB).

On the decibel scale, zero represents the lower limit of human hearing, 50 dB represents the level of a quiet conversation and 100 dB is a level of sound that can cause hearing loss if experienced over a long period of time.[14] A twofold increase of experienced sound is represented by an increase of 10 dB on the measurement scale. Since our ability to hear sounds drops off at high and low frequencies, sound intensity values at these wavelength ranges are sometimes reduced to reflect human ability to hear them. When they are reported in this way, they are called "A-weighted" decibels (dBA).

Sound waves have attributes similar to other waves: reflection, absorption, transmission, dispersion and refraction. Because they occupy the same space, sound waves from different sound sources and their associated reflections add together to create a combined total wave pattern. If they are synchronized with each other (in phase), they will combine to a larger waveform. If they are out of sync, they will interfere with each other and create a complex waveform similar to the chop that we see in ocean waves smashing up against a rocky shoreline and bouncing back. If they combine in such a way that the peak of one wave coincides with the trough of an equivalent frequency wave, they will cancel each other out and no sound is heard.

Though our whole bodies pick up low-frequency vibrations, our ears are our primary sound wave receptors. The outer ear serves as a funnel-like collector, directing sound waves toward the ear drum whose vibration sets tiny bones in the middle ear (the ossicles) in motion. These in turn amplify and transfer vibrations to the oval window which connects the middle ear and inner ear. From there, the vibrations enter the cochlea, a snail-shaped, fluid-filled organ. The vibrating fluid of the inner ear sets tiny nerve endings in motion, turning the vibrations into electrical impulses which travel along the auditory nerve to the brain. There, the overlapping waveforms from simultaneous sounds are decoded. This Rube Goldberg-type transfer of mechanical waves outside the body to intricately nuanced acoustic information is a wonder of the human sensory system.

UPON REFLECTION

Our experience of aural architecture is strongly affected by the reflection of sound waves off physical objects in a space. The reflections can be either specular (reflecting at the same angle as they initially hit the surface, as a mirror reflects light) or diffuse (dispersing in different directions so that the sound loses its directionality and is scattered like light bouncing off a rough surface). Each material has different characteristics of reflection, transmission, and absorption, and the proportion for each varies depending on the wavelength of the sound. Peter Zumthor calls this to mind as he urges us to

> "Listen! Interiors are like large instruments, collecting sound, amplifying it, transmitting it elsewhere. It has to do with the shape peculiar to each room and with the surfaces of the materials they contain and the way those materials have been applied."[15]

We can think of all these sounds and reflections as the voice of the building carrying on a conversation with us and providing information about the surfaces around us.

If we run down a flight of oak stairs in hard-soled shoes, the sound of our foot's impact on each step transmits out in all directions, and its intensity decreases the further it travels. Although some focused sounds project out in a specific direction, most sounds, like the footfall on the stair, are omnidirectional; that is, they radiate out from the sound source in concentric circles like ripples of water from a stone thrown into a pond. Upon encountering an object, such as an adjacent wall, the sound wave is absorbed, reflected and transmitted in proportions that depend on the object's material characteristics. The first sound wave we detect is the sound on its shortest path direct from the source to our ears. This initial sound and the reflections that closely follow it give us information about the direction of the sound. This information was critically important in our evolutionary development because it let us know if a predator was stalking us from the left or right side. So even today we react to these early sounds, instinctively turning our head in response to them if they are loud or unexpected.

The parts of the wave that don't travel directly to our ears hit surfaces and objects in the space around us, bounce off them and may eventually reach our ears through multiple reflections. Acoustic reflections can bounce around in a space for a long time so we first hear the direct sound and then, sometimes many seconds later, hear the reflections, each of which have taken a different path to our ears. The more reflective the materials in the space are, the more reflections are possible, creating a rich, full sound. This is called a "live" space and is the effect commonly enjoyed by those who sing in the shower, listen to Bach in a cathedral or delight in the sound of a water droplet in a dark cave.

Both early and later reflections carry information about the surfaces they've encountered on their journey toward our ears. The direction and clarity of reflected sound waves depend on the surface roughness relative to the sound wavelength. Flat planar surfaces, like polished marble, create coherent echoes at all wavelengths, while articulated, irregular surfaces disperse sound waves, especially at wavelengths similar to the irregularities in their surface texture.[16] Because low-frequency sound waves have a wavelength similar to the dimensions of architectural elements, they can bend around corners and objects in the space. They thus become more uniformly dispersed across space. Curved surfaces have special reflective properties. Concave surfaces focus sound at a point in space, while convex surfaces disperse it.[17] On the opposite side of a wall or an object's acoustic reflection is a sonic shadow, a space of relative quiet. Sonic shadows may be diffuse and blurred for low frequencies—which as we have noted, bend slightly around corners—or sharp and clear for higher frequencies.

Consciously or subliminally, our ears sound out the surfaces around us to sense these subtle differences and experience the acoustic ambiance of a place. We can more fully appreciate the contribution of reflections to the sonic feeling of a space by experiencing sound without them in a specially designed room that completely absorbs all reflections. These "anechoic" chambers are designed for research into acoustic parameters; for instance, to assess the performance of loudspeakers or the directional radiation of noise from industrial machinery. People who spend time in them report an eerie silence and suspension of time. George Michelson Foy, a novelist and essayist, visited one in his quest for the quietest place on Earth. He related that he

"had heard being in an anechoic chamber for longer than 15 minutes can cause extreme symptoms, from claustrophobia and nausea to panic attacks and aural hallucinations—you literally start hearing things. A violinist tried it and hammered on the door after a few seconds, demanding to be let out because he was so disturbed by the silence."[18]

Without its attendant reflections, the dimensional qualities of sound space flatten and time is suspended.

The texture of aural architecture depends on how the environment interacts with sound waves and changes their frequency mix (spectrum), amplitude, direction and temporal sequence. Sound often arrives simultaneously from all directions, an acoustic volume with no tangible borders. Yet our ears are skilled at tracing out the boundary of this sound space. The location of our ears on either side of our heads is an important aspect of how we evaluate it. Using this bilateral symmetry, we locate sounds by comparing the sound received from both sides. If a sound is louder in one ear than in the other, we learn over time to precisely evaluate the direction it comes from. If the sound is balanced on both sides no matter what direction we turn our head, then we experience being enveloped by a directionless sound.

At each reflection, some of the incident sound wave is absorbed by the reflecting surface, so the intensity of the wave diminishes over time. The amount of absorption depends on many characteristics of the surface material. In general, soft, porous materials are more absorptive and diminish sound more than hard, solid ones. For a given space, the time that it takes sound to diminish by 60 dB is called the reverberation time. In smaller, more absorptive spaces, the reverberation time may drop below 0.25 seconds. In a large, highly reflective space, like a Gothic cathedral, sound waves travel far between each reflection and the reverberation time may be 10 seconds or more. In this 10-second journey, the sound will have traveled 2 miles before dropping by 60 dB.[19] Thus it is the combination of time, reverberance and absorption that makes big rooms sound like big rooms and small rooms sound like small rooms. They also let us easily differentiate racquetball courts from plush upholstered living rooms.

We detect and interpret the time lag between the initial and reflected sounds differently depending on the amount of time between them. Short time lags of reflected sound that reach our ears within about 10 milliseconds of the initial sound fuse with the initial sound, making it appear louder. This is sometimes called the "Haas effect," named for the person who first identified it. Longer time lags may muddy the sound if we are trying to extract specific information from it, or they may provide a fullness of sound or "tonal coloration" if we are more interested in the flow of sound from tone to tone, as in music. Longer time lags of reflections from objects more than 33 ft (10 m) away can be experienced as an echo. In Greek mythology, these sounds represented the voice of Echo, a mountain nymph who loved the sound of her own voice.

As we can see, reverberance is not inherently good or bad, but it speaks to us about the surfaces around us and the volume of the space and has the power to enhance or destroy the sounds we experience. Long reverberation times immerse us in the full tonal color of a Gregorian chant but reduce the lyrics of a hip-hop song to an unintelligible garble. The inverse of reverberation is clarity, the ability to differentiate individual syllables or musical notes. As reverberation increases, clarity decreases. So in order to be understood, speech requires less reverberance; but to develop fullness, music requires more.

Because sound wavelengths are similar to the size of room dimensions, every room also has a sympathetic wavelength (or set of wavelengths) that is related to its physical dimensions of length, width and height. We may say the space is tuned to the resonant frequency (or frequencies) of this wavelength. When a tone at that frequency is played within the space, a synergy is created through additive interference between the original and reflecting sound waves, resulting in a significant increase in the sound intensity and reverberation time.

So every concert hall, classroom, diner or shower stall has its associated resonant frequency. Some spaces are accidentally or intentionally tuned to a single resonant frequency or a very narrow band of frequencies. This tuned resonance can have dramatic impacts, as Shea Trahan relates in his visit to the Oracle Chamber in the Hypogeum of Ħal-Saflieni on the island of Malta:

"Most important of all the chamber's characteristics is the fact that the people of this culture carved a perfect resonating chamber into solid stone. This was done over 5,000 years ago and accomplished with basic hand tools, somehow fine tuning the space to an undeniable resonant tone.

[…]

When the resonant frequency is reached (right at 110 Hz), a multisensory event takes place. The intensity of the sound of your voice within the space increases instantaneously, sounding as though someone has joined in singing. Additionally, the character of the sound becomes increasingly spatial, observably approaching you from all directions simultaneously and taking on a vibrotactile quality so that you sense the sound as a tingling vibration through the skin. When you discontinue singing the resonant tone, it remains notably audible for a few brief moments before decaying into silence. The experience is at once disorienting (you feel as though your equilibrium is lost) and awe inspiring.

[…]

More impressive though are the results of a study into the effects of the Hypogeum's particular frequency (110 Hz) upon the human brain. When the brain is exposed to the resonant frequency of the Hypogeum, the tone causes a shift in the prefrontal cortex from left dominance to right dominance. This shift de-activates the language centers of the brain (focused on rhythm and patterns) and hyperactivates the emotional center often associated with the perception of experiences of spirituality and enlightenment. It is believed that the Oracle Chamber's use by the shaman of this culture may have acted as a catalyst for mystical experience."[20]

As we see in the Oracle Chamber, a place's aural architecture (its resonant frequencies and reverberation characteristics) can invert the relationship between the space and the occupant. Rather than the occupant imposing sounds upon the space, sometimes the space actively directs the occupant toward particular sounds and tempos. In this way, our buildings become cultural determinants of the sounds within them. For example, the early Roman basilicas had long reverberation times of 5 to 10 seconds, causing reflections to fold back upon the following sounds. This degraded complex music and spoken words to an unintelligible, soupy mix of reverberations. Hence, the adoption of the slow, monophonic Gregorian chant as the dominant component of the Christian liturgy in these spaces (Figure 6.2).[21] Later, however, after the Protestant Reformation, smaller churches with shorter reverberation allowed a spoken liturgy to emerge.

This effect of buildings shaping the sound within them continues to influence us to the present day. Rock 'n' roll musician David Byrne's TED Talk on "How architecture helped music evolve" traces the ongoing impact of performance spaces on the music performed there. His exploration ranges from the minimal reverberation of early rock clubs and riverboat jazz venues to the "arena rock" of medium-speed ballads that has become the signature of rock groups as they transform their sound to fit the acoustics of a hockey arena.[22]

Figure 6.2 Hard surfaces and massive volumes of early Roman basilicas created long reverberation times. Renaissance revivals of these spaces, as in St. Peter's Basilica pictured above, have similar aural characteristics.

Shea Trahan's research into sound space takes this relationship a step further as he explores forms generated by sound alone. Trahan uses complex computer algorithms to generate three-dimensional shell-like "Nodal Structures" that embody the sonic waveform (Figure 6.3). Locating walls at the null point of the waveforms, Trahan creates spatial forms with the potential to manifest powerful sonic experiences. As Shea describes it, the walls effectively "bloom within the moments of calm inside a field of vibrating sonic energy."[23] His studies also show that tones with an audible harmonic relationship, such as a music triad, create similar structural forms. The organic forms generated have the potential to be habitable, hyper-resonant and reverberant spaces. They may be experienced as a sound bath or exploratorium, or they might be used as meditation chambers or laboratories for scientific studies of the impact of sound on brainwaves and consciousness. But for Shea, like the Hypogeum, they are in their essence magnificent temples of sound.

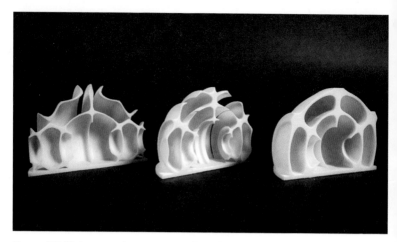

Figure 6.3 Using complex computer algorithms, Shea Trahan generates three-dimensional shell-like Nodal Structures that embody sonic waveforms. Note the similarities and progression of form for this A Minor triad.

THE GOOD, THE BAD, AND THE UGLY

No discussion of sound would be complete without addressing what we commonly call noise—all those unwanted sounds that get in the way of the sounds we want to hear (or the quiet that we want to experience). In fact, outside of the specialty of performance hall design, much of architectural acoustics design focuses on just this one aspect of sound—getting rid of noise.

Noise is basically just sound we don't want to hear, either because it doesn't match our current sound preferences or because it interferes with another sound that we are trying to hear. The noise may be anything from a consistent background hum of acoustic disturbance to sporadic loud outbursts of sound. Perhaps because apprehending environmental sounds was a critical survival mechanism in human evolution, noisy disturbances can cause us stress even at low levels. A study in the late 1990s compared stress levels (as measured by cortisol levels in the body) of experienced female clerical workers in a quiet versus a more noisy office with a low-intensity buzz common to many open-plan offices. The workers in the noisy office had stress hormone levels significantly higher than those in the quiet office and also showed signs of reduced motivation.[24] The opposite effect may also happen where soothing background sounds reduce stress.

What we call noise differs from person to person (ask anyone with a teenager) and from time to time. In general, we consider a sound annoying if it is unpredictable, unnecessary, or created by someone or something that we're either not involved with or have an unfavorable attitude toward. Noise is measured in decibels, the same as appreciated sounds. Our ability to hear a sound of interest (the signal) is described by the "signal-to-noise ratio," the ratio between the intensity of the desired sound and that of the background (undesirable) noise.

Noise travels through air and, thus, can slip through any opening in an enclosed environment. Noise also is transmitted through the solid elements of an enclosure, which is an especially important channel for low-frequency sounds as we noted earlier. As for any sound, we have three opportunities to control noise—at the source, along its path of travel and at the receiver (the person hearing it). At the source, we either reduce its amplitude or isolate it by moving it far away from other activities. Along its path, we can control its projection by carefully designing the location of walls and surfaces, the absorption and transmission characteristics of their materials, and the shape and location of openings through which it might travel. We can also camouflage noise by introducing other sounds/frequencies that either mask its presence (like the use of white noise in an office setting or a waterfall in a landscape) or cancel it out (see Figures 6.4 and 6.5).

Figures 6.4 and 6.5 Waterfall Garden Park is a small (4,800 ft²/446 m²) pocket park in Seattle's densely developed downtown. Unassuming from the exterior (top photo), the enveloping sound of a raging waterfall inside (bottom photo) masks the intense traffic sounds of the streets around it, creating a natural haven amidst the urban density (Sasaki, Dawson and DeMay, 1977).

The receiver (the person detecting the sound) has options to move away, turn their head or ignore the sound and attend to other sounds or to put on earplugs or headphones to effectively block it. As Blesser and Salter remind us, "headphones are the new wall."[25]

THE BUILDING'S VOICE

A YouTube video[26] shows Daniel Kish riding a bicycle and hiking in the woods without a guide. It's not a remarkable feat until you realize that Daniel is totally blind. Kish was born with retinoblastoma, an aggressive form of cancer which attacks the retinas. As a life-saving measure, both of his eyes were removed by the time he was 13 months old. He hears his way through the world by making verbal clicking sounds with his tongue and interpreting their reflections off adjacent surfaces. It wasn't until the mid-twentieth century that researchers clearly identified that it was this auditory skill of echolocation that allowed blind people to navigate space without vision.[27] A self-trained world expert in echolocation, Daniel demonstrates how an echo off a wall can be perceived as either a sound or a wall. Most of us will hear it as a sound, but with practice, we can understand it as a wall and switch back and forth between these two perceptual frameworks.[28]

Daniel's ability is a remarkable example of something that we all do at a subliminal level every day. Sighted people also register sound reflections to provide cues about the surrounding environment. These reflected and absorbed sounds give spaces their auditory personality. Our education about the acoustic environments we inhabit is woven into the flow of life itself, whether it is experiencing a mother's lullaby while still in utero, subliminally sensing the narrowness of an office building corridor or being immersed in an Afro-Cuban beat at a local club. We learn to associate reverberation and engulfing sound with enclosed space, echoes with remote surfaces, low frequencies with soft objects and higher frequencies with hard objects. Usually this is not a conscious process; and we don't have a well-developed vocabulary to express its effect. Frequently, we report it as an emotional mood (I feel relaxed, happy, nervous) or bodily symptom (goosebumps, muscle tightness) or just register it as an unconscious bodily change like an increase or decrease in blood pressure.[29]

In general, hard, dense, smooth surfaces, like concrete, reflect more of the incoming sound waves (up to 99 percent). Perhaps because these attributes match those of a thermal conductor, these surfaces are often called acoustically "cold." On the other hand, surfaces that are porous, soft, rough, fibrous and lightweight, like a thick carpet or a good insulating material, absorb most of the sound wave, so we often describe these absorptive materials as acoustically "warm." A highly absorptive space is also frequently called "dead" because of its tendency to deaden sound within it; and by contrast, a reflective space is called "live."

Absorption of sound waves also increases when a material is in direct contact with an air space that acts to absorb some of the wavelength energy. Coupled air spaces are frequently used to tune the acoustics for performance halls. The softness and hardness (or warmness/coldness) describes the tonal color of the space. Juhani Pallasmaa acknowledges this personality of acoustic space as he notes

"We can recall the acoustic harshness of an uninhabited and unfurnished house as compared to the affability of a lived home in which sound is refracted and softened by the surfaces of numerous objects of personal life. Every building or space has its characteristic sound of intimacy or monumentality, rejection or invitation, hospitality or hostility."[30]

As with any experience we are immersed within, it is difficult to talk about acoustic space from a single perspective. So below, we'll look at this space from four different angles: the active interaction between our bodies and the building; the perspective of the individual hearing the space (the sound "horizon"); the experience of the group engulfed in a single sound space (the sound "arena"); and the effect of iconic sounds in the soundscape ("soundmarks"). Although we may not all become trained in echolocation or the scientific specifics of acoustic reflections, we can learn to hear the unique voice of the acoustic environments we inhabit. We can experience their shape and intensity and recognize our reaction to them; and we can use this embodied experience to guide our design process.

CONVERSING WITH A BUILDING

Architecturally, sound space is the one sensory space that's activated by the presence of people and animals. We speak to a building with each motion and vocalization we make within it, and we hear its response. A person bounds down the stairs and the stairs speak back—sometimes with the soft murmur of bare feet on carpet, sometimes with the sharp staccato of high heels on polished wood. The sound depends on how both occupant and architecture are dressed. Blesser and Salter point out the personality that the acoustic voice gives to a setting:

"Metaphorically, the reverberated sound of footsteps is the reactive voice of the space; the spatial acoustics of a reverberant space announce the presence of active life by responding with an audible hello, as either a whisper or a shout. The acoustics are like the voice of a receptionist, with aural architects determining how that voice should greet entering visitors."[31]

Peter Zumthor is a master at attending to this interaction. The Saint Benedict Chapel he designed in the village of Sumvitg, for example, is a pointed wedge of dark, shingled wood whose interior resembles a ship's galley. The floor creaks here, and Zumthor admits that it is on purpose. He intentionally warped the floor slightly to create the creak, which exists just below the level of consciousness, adding a small, memorable accent to the voice of this building.[32]

To investigate this interaction in my sensory design class at the University of Washington, I ask students to sit in a side hallway in Architecture Hall, a location which has little visual connection with the spaces of the building, and listen to this conversation between occupants and the building. Constructed for the Alaska–Yukon–Pacific Exposition in 1909, Architecture Hall is a 48,000 ft^2 (4,459 m^2) building with a large, open interior stairway that connects three floors of classrooms and studios. Students are instructed to write down the sounds they hear, recording the character of the sound (frequency, tempo, information content, etc.), the source (if they can identify it), its intensity and their response to it (like/ dislike). To summarize their impressions from the exercise, I ask them to describe the voice of the building as if it were a person interacting with its occupants. The descriptions vary widely, but a clear personality emerges as some repeated phrases capture the conversation between this hard-surfaced building and its young, active occupants. The descriptive words students use to characterize the building's conversation with its occupants include *impatient, irritated, stressed, fast-paced, boisterous, on edge, short-tempered, crisp and decisive, a bit anxious*, and

Acoustic Space

schizophrenic. Architecture Hall is obviously not a place of rest. This exercise is the start of a week-long investigation into sound space that sensitizes students to the life of the soundscape around them.

HORIZON AND ARENA

In *Spaces Speak, Are You Listening?*, Blesser and Salter discuss the spatial aspects of the soundscape from two different perspectives. The first of these, the horizon, is centered on the listener and represents the farthest horizon of space within which the listener receives sound.[33] The second, the arena, centers on the sound source and includes the area within which a group of listeners can hear a particular sonic event. Thus, these two concepts describe overlapping sound volumes from the different perspectives of the generator and the perceiver. For a group of people telling stories around a campfire, the acoustic horizon for a listener might consist of an irregular volume of sound that includes the sound of the storyteller within the circle plus the laughter from an adjacent boisterous campsite and the distant drone of a waterfall across the valley at the farthest reach of their hearing. The acoustic arena for the story circle, on the other hand, is a sphere of sound centered on the campfire which, depending on how loud the storytellers are, may extend only 6–10 ft (2–3 m) away from the person telling the story. People beyond that distance are outside the listening boundary and would not be able to hear the stories.

We alternate between these two perspectives (arena and horizon) of soundspace as we regulate our voices to moderate the size of our own arena, adjusting how far we can be heard, and as we send out the tentacles of our listening to probe the horizon of the sound world that surrounds us. The form and materials of the built environment affect each of these as it reflects, absorbs and masks the sounds around us.

As we've noted, sound moves in complex ways. It bounces against walls and bends around corners and lets us probe into and be a part of unseen spaces. We can hear the echo of a footfall on a floor above us and be aware of both the distant space where the sound occurred and the connecting space between us, whether it is the transmission through a solid floor or the reflection down a stairwell. As our listening ears probe the acoustic horizon, we are like an octopus reaching its tentacles far into the innards of a building. The student exercise in Architecture Hall is one example of exploring this horizon from a single location in the building. Since we judge the size of a space partially based on this experienced sound horizon, we can also use it to alter our perception of size. For example, muffling the sound of a waterfall in a Japanese garden can make it seem farther away, thus enlarging the perceived size of the garden.[34]

Most soundscapes are a combination of directional and enveloping sound. The shape of the acoustic horizon is affected by the relative strength of each. The native environment we evolved in had low sonic reflections and thus did not provide enveloping reverberations. Its acoustic horizon was dominated by directional sounds, giving survival information about the presence of predators whose exact location we could then confirm with our eyes. Today we are still influenced by this primal tension when we can't determine where a sound comes from. The 1949 movie *The Third Man* used this primitive reflex to increase suspense in one of its classic chase scenes. In the movie, the antagonist, Harry Lime, is being pursued like a cornered rat through the underground sewers of Vienna. He can hear his pursuers, but he can't see them.

Intense echoes of their shouts and footfalls probe the horizon of soundspace, molding a stark and convoluted understanding of the labyrinth of hollow pipes surrounding him. The highly reflective tunnel walls amplify the sound but conceal the exact location of his pursuers. Director Carol Reed edits the chase into long, echoing, empty sewer vistas and close-ups of Lime's sweaty face as his eyes dart around searching for an escape.[35]

In contrast to the sound horizon, a sound arena is centered on a sound-making entity and encompasses the bubble of space within which a particular sound can be heard. Depending on the aural architecture, the shape of an arena may be symmetrical or directional and may have variations of intensity within it. An acoustic arena usually falls off gradually at the edges unless it is enclosed by walls or is tightly focused to a directional acoustic shape. The form and materials of the world around us distort the shape of these sound spaces, as do the aural characteristics of the sound generated and the hearing abilities of the perceivers.

The ratio of sound to noise in a space contributes to the size and shape of its arenas. In order to be included within an arena, a listener must be able to hear the sound above the background noise. The relative intensities of the meaningful sound and the noise in a space define the edges of communication, the boundary beyond which conveyed messages deteriorate. Silence creates large acoustic arenas, while a high level of background noise shrinks arenas. By changing the ratio of target sound to unwanted noise, a designer changes the size and shape of the sound arenas. Materials that absorb the target sound decrease the signal and thus decrease its arena. For example, in a large hotel, a polished granite entry floor speaks both to the upscale atmosphere and to the public nature of the space. The sharp tapping of footsteps echoing along it draws attention from a large arena and says that this is a public space. The adjacent carpeted sitting area with its plush upholstery, on the other hand, speaks to a more private setting where arenas are smaller and intimate conversations may remain confidential.[36]

As we have seen, curved walls can focus sound, thus extending an arena in one direction while shrinking it in another to create hot spots or dead spots. The whispering gallery at St. Paul's Cathedral in London is a popular example of the ability of space to focus sound. A whisper at one point along the curved walls of the central dome at St. Paul's is carried by waves that travel around the circumference clinging to the walls. Thus a person whispering on one side of the circular gallery can be heard quite clearly on the other side some 138 ft (42 m) away.

Acoustic arenas don't necessarily respect visual boundaries and may have a very different shape than the building's physical geometry. They can shrink down to a subset of the tectonic space or expand to include areas outside the identified space. For example, the sound arena for teens playing rock music in their bedroom may leak out around (or through) a closed door or open window to include other parts of the house or even the neighbor's backyard and house. The arena may expand or contract with the opening and closing of doors, as noted by the article in *The New York Times* about restaurant acoustics that reminds us: "Make no mistake, New York City will always have brasseries and pizzerias and saloons that generate the sort of sonic pandemonium that pours out onto the sidewalk like ice water from a bucket when you open the front door."[37]

Both soft, absorbent surfaces and high levels of background noise shrink arenas, allowing people to adjust their personal arena by modulating their voice level and direction of speech. If the speaker faces a person and talks loudly enough, that person will be included in their arena; but if the speaker turns away or whispers, they can effectively exclude a person from their arena.[38] When arenas are small, more of them can occupy the same tectonic space, as is demonstrated by cozy restaurants that modulate background noise to make each set of diners feel like they are in their own private acoustic world. Noting an increased awareness of this aural architecture, the article from *The New York Times* points out that "restaurant designers are becoming more precise and scientific, working to create self-enclosed huddles of talk at each table without losing the low rumble of activity that makes a place feel alive"[39] (Figure 6.6).

Reflective surfaces, on the other hand, act like amplifiers to enlarge an arena or intensify it in certain areas or directions. We have also seen that they can increase or decrease the intelligibility or fidelity of a sound depending on the aural architecture and its associated reverberation time. Most performance halls are carefully designed to maintain the fidelity of either the spoken voice or music across the whole audience seating area. But still there will be variations across the space and some positions will have better sound than others. If you visit a music venue, the resident director will probably be able to point out the "king's seat"—the one where the acoustics are most perfect.

All of these decisions about the size and shape of acoustic arenas and horizons have impacts on our behavior. Arenas, by definition, represent acoustic "rooms" that enclose social groupings linked by sound. The acoustic arena of a church bell often defined the extent of the village or the local parish. It used to be said that to be a true Londoner or Cockney, you had to

Figure 6.6 Fabric banners in this colorful Mediterranean restaurant help reduce reverberation and shape the acoustic arena for the dining area.

be born within the sound of the bells of St. Mary-le-Bow church (the Bow bells). But these days, noise pollution is drowning out the sound of the bells and has shrunk their audio arena to about one-twentieth of its original size. Currently there are no maternity wards within earshot of St. Mary-le-Bow's bells, effectively ending this lineage of true Londoners.[40]

With the electronic communications of today, we are less defined by these acoustic boundaries, yet the geometry of acoustic arenas and horizons still shapes our social interactions. We still modulate sound volumes to define social territories. Just as a church bell in a tenth-century village defined the territory of the village citizenry, so a whispered comment at a party defines the private social dimension of inclusion and exclusion.

SOUND MARKS THE SPOT

Sometimes sounds in the built environment develop a special meaning over time or are engineered to provide special information about the locale. A bell may signal the arrival of a customer in a store, or a siren might signal a warning of impending danger. At the time of the Samurai, Japanese craftsmen intentionally designed floors to squeak in order to alert the occupants to intruders. Sometimes these iconic sounds simply mark a particular location. At the Cedar River Watershed Education Center near Seattle (Figure 6.7), water from rain and computer-activated drippers falls onto drums located in the central courtyard, creating the haunting sound of drumming that permeates the site and draws visitors to its center.

When sounds are used in this way, they are called "soundmarks" or "earcons" (a sound icon).[41] Rather than experiencing ourselves within their arena, we see them as markers in the soundscape and gauge our position relative to their sonic location. Both terms are similar and often used interchangeably, but there are subtle differences. Soundmarks are touchstones on an environment that represent sounds that come to be identified with a particular place or region. For example, the sound of waves is a soundmark that lets us know we are near a seashore. Earcons are similar, but they carry symbolic meaning or meta-information about the world. A wind chime is an earcon that lets us know the wind is blowing. Frequently, symbolic sounds are experienced as both a soundmark

Figure 6.7 The haunting sound of drumming greets visitors to the Cedar River Watershed Education Center (North Bend, WA). But the source of this drumming is not revealed until they reach Seattle artist Dan Corson's Rain Drum Courtyard where water from rain and computer-activated drippers create a memorable musical event.

and an earcon, as when the peal from a bell tower both marks the center of a university campus and provides information about the time of day.

Both soundmarks and earcons animate the soundscape and can make a place special and memorable. Sometimes these acoustic events are at a grand scale and become synonymous with an entire locale, as in the sound of Big Ben that has come to stand for the whole of London. But others mark simple, everyday events like the scraping of heavy metal chairs on tile floors of coffeehouses in Paris or the drumbeat of rain on a metal roof in Ethiopia. The pioneering sound artist Matthew Herbert made a list of the ten best sounds his house makes. Among them, he describes a humble cow bell.

"Our back gate is out of sight from the house, but I hung a cow bell on it so you can hear when someone opens or closes it. The bell I found though is handmade and roughly forged. Amazingly, it has the loudest, clearest tone of a bell I've heard of that size. I love hearing it ping so elegantly in the evening as I know it means my wife has returned home from work."[42]

Earcons may consist of either unique sonic events or unusual spatial acoustics. Any form of memorable acoustics, whether intentional or accidental, coupled with a specific locale can with repeated exposure become associated with the meaning of a particular place. The whispering gallery at St. Paul's Cathedral that focuses sound allowing whispers to be heard across the dome, the acoustic drinking fountains in the Seattle airport that gurgle with anticipation as someone leans in to drink, the chirping echo of a quetzal bird that calls out from the steps of the 1,100-year-old Mayan Temple of Kukulcan when you clap your hands in front of them—all of these are earcons that connect us with place. Many of them have become tourist attractions that appear on sound tourism websites like Sonic Wonders,[43] a travel guide to the sound world authored by Trevor Cox, Professor of Acoustic Engineering at the University of Salford. This site lets the armchair traveler sample the acoustic soundmarks and earcons of the world and includes everything from a sea organ in Zadar, Croatia, to a singing road in Hokkaido, Japan.

ACOUSTIC DESIGNERS AND THEIR TOOLS

Outside of performance halls and event venues, few buildings have a clearly identified acoustic designer who shapes the aural architecture beyond what is necessary to combat identified noise problems. Indeed, the science of acoustics is relatively new and, until recently, relied heavily on trial and error or copying the design of an earlier space.

The earliest writings on acoustics were those of Vitruvius (30 BC). In his *Book V*, he presented an extensive discussion of acoustic principles informed by the use of ray tracing to demonstrate the location of acoustic shadows.[44] But progress from there was slow, and it wasn't until the late nineteenth century that Wallace Clement Sabine merged the theoretical physics and math understandings of sound with the empirical measurement of space. Sabine's exploration of sonic space was a labor of rigor and determination. Sabine was only a junior faculty member in the Harvard Department of Physics when he took on the task of remedying the acoustical problems in the lecture room of the university's Fogg Art Museum—a task that more senior faculty sidestepped, thinking it was impossibly difficult. Sabine spent two years taking rigorous measurements that compared this room with Sander's Theater, another Harvard building with excellent acoustics. In the course of this work, he developed a quantitative understanding of the reverberation, absorption and sound transmittance in the space. This accomplishment established Sabine's reputation as the "father" of modern architectural acoustics and led to his selection as acoustical consultant for Boston's Symphony Hall, constructed in 1900 and generally considered one of the best symphony halls in the world.[45]

This innovative work had unforeseen impacts as it ushered in an unprecedented era for control of the soundscape. The engineering work that ensued both identified noise and reverberations as culprits hindering the propagation of pure, clean sound and gave architects and sound engineers the materials and tools to rid interior soundscapes of background noise and unwanted reverberations. Dr. Emily Thompson traces this evolution in her book *The Soundscape of Modernity*, noting several technical innovations that shaped it. The first was the development of a wide range of new sound-absorbing materials that dramatically dampened reflections, achieving "Control Through Absorption."[46] The new materials included plant fibers, cork, felt, mineral wool and asbestos. Their development led eventually to the ubiquitous T-bar dropped ceiling acoustic tiles. These materials dampened sound in buildings from major concert halls to kindergarten playrooms. The headquarters building for the New York Life Insurance Company, built in 1929, incorporated over ten acres of sound-absorbing felt material, more than any other building in the world. The second innovation was the use of amplified (and eventually digitized) sound that did not depend on room characteristics for transmission. The listening public was also transformed by these changes as non-reverberant sounds were fed directly to the ears, allowing individuals to become more attuned to the acoustic clarity. What was lost in reverberant fullness was reintroduced electronically to generate a perfect reverberant sound that was completely disconnected from the space that held it.[47] The new sound was considered efficient, productive and placeless. Many of our current environments still reflect this sonic anonymity.

But today, aural architects have a choice in the design of the soundscape and a wide range of tools to predict sound performance before a space is constructed. Scale model studies with miniature sound sources and receivers can be used to represent sound in space. But more often, commercial software is used to simulate the movement and reflection of sound in a space. These simulations are then combined with recorded sounds to produce a virtual reality experience of the sound. For example, the architecture and engineering firm Arup has a series of Sound Labs that allow designers and their clients to listen to a building space before it's built—equivalent to a virtual tour of the building's sound. First, they capture the aural architecture of the room; then they record "dry" sounds (recorded in an anechoic chamber without any reflection) that might be common to the proposed space. The sound of the space is then "auralized" by 12 speakers that encircle the occupant and reproduce the strength and reflections of the sound waves in the space, letting designers and clients experience what a room would sound like.[48] These techniques clearly cross over into the realm of virtual reality and gaming, and the field of architecture is benefiting greatly from the talent and research investments being made in these areas.

THE INNER BEING

From the echo of a Gothic cathedral to vocalizations arising from deep within our bodies, sound gives voice to the mysterious interior world. We don't stand separate from this voice, but are immersed within its resonance like a pearl diver surrounded by water. This resonant voice of the world has fascinated mankind, starting with the mystery and sacredness of the voice of the cave spirit. Some of the earliest animal drawings have been found in resonant caves that were sonic hot spots. Sacred spaces also occurred near lithophones—natural stalactites and stalagmites that produce sounds like a marimba.[49] In fact, it was not until 350 BC that Aristotle identified sound as a physical rather than a mystical entity. And, as Murray Schafer points out: "It was not until the Renaissance that God became portraiture. Previously He had been conceived as sound or vibration."[50]

As it vibrates around us, sound has the power to raise us to an altered state of ecstasy or drop us into a primal panic. Hence Blesser and Salter refer to the aural architect as a modern-day shaman with the power to transform our experience in the spaces around us.[51] This will not be accomplished with numbers and simulations alone. We must first regain our ability to hear the soundscape anew. This can only be done by slowing down and fully experiencing the sound around us, feeling how it moves our emotions, noticing how it draws people together or separates them out, sensing how it moves us forward or holds us stationary, noting how it speaks to the familiar, the sacred or the busy life of the city. The world of sound is the true classroom of the aural architect.

As aural architects, we have control over the dimensions, shape, texture and materials of the built environment. Designing these, we shape acoustic arenas and determine the extent to which adjacent conversations will join or remain private. We contribute to the comfort and confidence of people with compromised vision or people moving through a space with low illumination. We determine the degree to which the occupants experience sound as if it were coming from a distant open window or as an enveloping medium. As we shape these experiences in the world of sound, perhaps at times we may also evoke the inner voice of the sacred.

Notes

1   Juhani Pallasmaa, *The Eyes of the Skin: Architecture and the Senses* (West Sussex: John Wiley & Sons, 2005), 50.
2   R. Murray Schafer, *The Soundscape: Our Sonic Environment and the Tuning of the World* (Rochester, Vermont: Destiny, 1994 [1977]).
3   Victoria Meyers, *Invisible Buildings*, www.victoriameyers.com/page/2/, (accessed November 17, 2015).
4   See, for example, Purdue University's Record the Earth project by Bryan Pijanowski at https://www.recordtheearth.org/ and the University of Salford's Sound Around You project at www.soundaroundyou.com/
5   Shea Trahan, "TED Talk: the architecture of sound," *YouTube*, October 13, 2015 [video], https://www.youtube.com/watch?v=R-BMF4e-1bg
6   See, for example, Marshall Long, *Architectural Acoustics*, 2nd Edition (Oxford: Academic Press, 2014); William J. Cavanaugh and Gregory C. Tocci, *Architectural Acoustics: Principles and Practice* (New Jersey: John Wiley & Sons, 2010).
7   Michael Kimmelman, "Dear architects: sound matters," *The New York Times*, Critic's Notebook, December 29, 2015, www.nytimes.com/

interactive/2015/12/29/arts/design/sound-architecture.html?hp&action=c
lick&pgtype=Homepage&clickSource=story-heading&module=photo-spot-
region&region=top-news&WT.nav=top-news

8   Barry Blesser and Linda-Ruth Salter, *Spaces Speak, Are You Listening?*
    (Cambridge: The MIT Press, 2009), 15.
9   Ibid., 16 and private communications with Barry Blesser.
10 Blesser and Salter, *Spaces Speak, Are You Listening?*, 79–80.
11 "Immersed, sound and architecture," *OASE* 78 (2009), www.oasejournal.nl/en/
    Issues/78
12 Bea Goller, "Sound as space generator," *Architecture and Sound Research*,
    https://sonomorphism.wordpress.com/writings/sound-as-space-generator/
    (accessed February 21, 2016).
13 Michael Ermann, *Architectural Acoustics Illustrated* (Hoboken: John Wiley &
    Sons, 2015), 14.
14 Ibid., 5
15 Peter Zumthor, *Atmospheres* (Basel: Birkhauser, 2006), 29.
16 David A. Bies and Colin H. Hansen, *Engineering Noise Control: Theory and
    Practice*, 4th Edition (London: Spon Press, 2009), 327.
17 Blesser and Salter, *Spaces Speak, Are You Listening?*, 337.
18 George Michelson Foy, "Experience: I've been to the quietest place on Earth,"
    The Guardian, May 18, 2012, www.theguardian.com/lifeandstyle/2012/
    may/18/experience-quietest-place-on-earth
19 Ermann, *Architectural Acoustics Illustrated*, 62.
20 "Resonant form: the convergence of sound and space," *Shea Trahan*, www.
    sheatrahan.com/#!project-1/c1o27 (accessed July 20, 2016).
21 Blesser and Salter, *Spaces Speak, Are You Listening?*, 92.
22 David Byrne, "How architecture helped music evolve," *TED*, February 2010,
    [video], https://www.ted.com/talks/david_byrne_how_architecture_helped_
    music_evolve?language=en#t-593858 (accessed July 20, 2016).
23 Shea Trahan, "Resonant form."
24 Ermann, *Architectural Acoustics Illustrated*, 152.
25 Blesser and Salter, *Spaces Speak, Are You Listening?*, 161.
26 "Blind as a bat: seeing without eyesight," *YouTube*, July 18, 2011 [video], www.
    youtube.com/watch?v=Z_E3zxx2l9g
27 Blesser and Salter, *Spaces Speak, Are You Listening?*, 37.
28 Ibid., 14.
29 Ibid., 324.
30 Juhani Pallasmaa, "An architecture of the seven senses," in *Questions of
    Perception*, ed. Steven Holl, Juhani Pallasmaa, and Alberto Pérez-Gómez (San
    Francisco: William Stout Publishers, 2006), 30.
31 Blesser and Salter, *Spaces Speak, Are You Listening?*, 62–3.
32 Michael Kimmelman, "The ascension of Peter Zumthor," *The New York Times
    Magazine*, March 11, 2011, www.nytimes.com/2011/03/13/magazine/mag-
    13zumthor-t.html?ref=michaelkimmelman&_r=0
33 Blesser and Salter, *Spaces Speak, Are You Listening?*, 22.
34 Ibid., 66.
35 "Reviews: *The Third Man*," *Roger Ebert*, December 8, 1996, www.rogerebert.
    com/reviews/great-movie-the-third-man-1949
36 Blesser and Salter, *Spaces Speak, Are You Listening?*, 3.
37 Jeff Gordinier, "Restaurants take the din out of dining," *The New York Times*,
    September 4, 2015, www.nytimes.com/2015/09/09/dining/restaurants-
    noise-acoustics.html?ribbon-ad-idx=4&src=me&module=Ribbon&vers
    ion=origin&region=Header&action=click&contentCollection=Most%20
    Emailed&pgtype=article
38 Blesser and Salter, *Spaces Speak, Are You Listening?*, 28.

39   Gordinier, "Restaurants take the din out of dining."
40   Chris Parsons, "Could Cockneys soon be brown bread?" *Daily Mail*, June 26, 2012, www.dailymail.co.uk/news/article-2164799/Bow-Bells-mark-area-true-Londoners-drowned-capitals-noise-pollution.html#ixzz3qvu35k00
41   Blesser and Salter, *Spaces Speak, Are You Listening?*, 82–4.
42   Matthew Herbert, "The 10 best sounds that my house makes," *DUMMY*, www.dummymag.com/lists/the-10-best-sounds-that-my-house-makes-by-matthew-herbert
43   Sound Tourism: A Sonic Guide to Sonic Wonders, www.sonicwonders.org/ (accessed July 20, 2016).
44   Blesser and Salter, *Spaces Speak, Are You Listening?*, 80.
45   Ibid., 78.
46   Emily Thompson, *The Soundscape of Modernity: Architectural Acoustics and the Culture of Listening in America, 1900–1933* (Cambridge: The MIT Press, 2004), 191.
47   Ibid., 2–4.
48   Raj Patel, "The Arup SoundLab," *Arup*, [video], www.arup.com/Services/Acoustic_Consulting/SoundLab_Overview.aspx (accessed July 20, 2016).
49   Blesser and Salter, *Spaces Speak, Are You Listening?*, 74–5.
50   Murray Schafer, *The Soundscape*, 10.
51   Blesser and Salter, *Spaces Speak, Are You Listening?*, 73.

Olfactory Space

Chapter 7

"Cities are smells ... Cairo is the smell of mango and ginger. Beirut is the smell of the sun, sea, smoke, and lemons. Paris is the smell of fresh bread, cheese, and derivations of enchantment. Damascus is the smell of jasmine and dried fruit. Tunis is the smell of night musk and salt. Rabat is the smell of henna, incense, and honey. A city that cannot be known by its smell is unreliable."[1]

Mahmoud Darwish

"There's no there, there," Gertrude Stein once said of Oakland, California, San Francisco's rival shipping port across San Francisco Bay. But that was never said of Tacoma, Seattle's shipping counterpart across Puget Sound. There was definitely something there, and as my grandma used to say, "It stunk to high heaven." The "Aroma of Tacoma," as it was known to area locals, was a putrid stench, likened to the odor of rotten eggs. The nickname dates back to the 1940s but the smell was famous well before that in the early 1900s. The aroma has been attributed to a number of causes, including sediment in Commencement Bay, one of the most polluted bodies of water in the United States. But most of it came from the crown of industrial smokestacks that puncture the skyline along its tidelands. A stew of airborne contaminants, including sulfur released from the Simpson Tacoma Kraft paper mill, spilled from these, giving the city its iconic olfactory tag line.[2] Tacoma's smell was notorious. It made rock star Bruce Springsteen so sick on a concert tour that he had to leave town early. It threatened the city's commercial vitality and tourism industry. Mitigation efforts at the paper mill in the early 2000s substantially reduced the famous aroma, yet still the reputation remains in the jokes of visitors, the memories of residents and even a mocking song refrain:

"The Aroma of Tacoma takes your breath away.
You can tell it, you can smell it, when you're fourteen miles away!
From the great Olympic Mountains to the tide flats by the shore,
that aroma will be with us for now and ever more!"[3]

THE SENSESCAPE OF MEMORY

Smell is a troubled and underappreciated sense. Smell has been called a "primitive, animal, instinctual, voluptuous, erotic, egoistic, impertinent, libertine, frivolous and asocial sense."[4] It's also been called the least valuable sense—the first one people would sacrifice if forced to choose among the senses.[5]

The olfactory terrain is charted by the "smellscape," a term first used in 1990 by geographer J. Douglas Porteous in his book *Landscapes of the Mind: Worlds of Senses and Metaphor*.[6] We are generally somewhat oblivious to this smellscape around us. Since we breathe in and out more than 20,000 times a day, it would be distracting if we consciously registered all the aromas we took in. So our minds have a filtering mechanism that lets us ignore most smells in the air. We usually only notice odors when they are strong, unfamiliar or especially pleasant or unpleasant. The rest of the time, we unfairly assume that odors are unimportant.[7]

Yet, odors are an essential part of our connection with the atmosphere or ambiance of place as well as being a formidable motivator. They are closely associated with memory and the deep well of our emotions. Just one whiff of a scent that resides in our olfactory history has the power to excite our earliest memories and transport us to places halfway around the world. Avery Gilbert, a smell scientist and author of the book *What the Nose Knows*, explains the immediacy of this connection. For "every other sense," he says, "the information has to take a detour through the thalamus to reach the cerebral cortex. And smell has a privileged fast lane, right to the cortex."[8] Via this shortcut, smell travels to two centers in the brain that are essential for generating memories and emotion: the amygdala and the hippocampus. As Gilbert puts it, "right away, even just by the sheer wiring diagram of smell, we're talking about emotion and memory."[9]

Not only does the sense of smell exert this primal pull, but since it is tied to the very breath of life, smell, like touch, is a sense that we cannot voluntarily turn off. Patrick Süskind poetically reminds us of this in his novel *Perfume: The Story of a Murderer*:

> "People could close their eyes to greatness, to horrors, to beauty, and their ears to melodies or deceiving words. But they could not escape scent. For scent was a brother to breath. Together with breath it entered human beings, who could not defend themselves against it, not if they wanted to live. And scent enters into their very core, went directly to their hearts, and decided for good and all between affection and contempt, disgust and lust, love and hate."[10]

However, in our modern world, odors are heavily controlled, and this sensory aspect of our built environment is more often addressed as "air quality" with the assumption that all identifiable odors have been removed. The sanitization of the local smellscape is evident from the personal scale of our bodies to the urban scale of entire neighborhoods. This approach to a sensory realm is equivalent to taking all the flavor and texture out of food and replacing it with chemical nutrients in a tasteless paste.

THE NOSE KNOWS

Smell is one of our chemical senses. These are probably the most primitive of our sensory systems. Even one-celled bacteria and amoeba have chemoreceptors that draw them to beneficial chemicals and help them avoid harmful ones in their environment. Smell is also closely tied to taste, one of our body's other chemoreceptor senses.

The physiology of the sense of smell remained a relative mystery until recently. Not until the Nobel Prize-winning work of Linda Buck and Richard Axel in 1991 did the scientific community come to some agreement about how our sense of smell works.[11] Everything we smell is a chemical with molecules arranged in different ways. Our noses are really the antechamber, a virtual loading dock for air and odors. As air is sucked down into the lungs, olfactory signals race up to the brain.[12] For a substance to smell, it must be volatile (able to evaporate so that it becomes airborne). As we breathe in, these airborne molecules are drawn to the top of the nose, or olfactory cleft. There, they dissolve in a mucus membrane known as the olfactory epithelium that contains millions of sensory neurons. Although some competing vibrational resonance theories are emerging, the current scientific understanding is that the tips of these cells contain protein receptors that bind with odor molecules in an interaction similar to a lock and key.[13] The receptors are the locks; the keys to open them are the odor molecules that float past. Humans have about 450 different types of these olfactory receptors, which seems like a lot until you realize that dogs have twice as many. Each receptor type can be activated by many different odor molecules, and each odor molecule activates several different types of receptors.

We need only eight molecules of substance to trigger an impulse of smell in a nerve ending.[14] When an odor molecule activates a receptor, it generates a signal that is passed along tiny nerve fibers to the olfactory bulb in the brain, which in turn transmits information to other parts of the brain for further processing. Part of this processing integrates smell information with taste information, thus contributing strongly to our sense of taste. Other processing occurs in sections of the brain that are relatively old in evolutionary terms. These primitive structures operate more instinctually and regulate our emotion, memory and motivation. The olfactory bulb has relatively weak links to the most recently developed parts of the brain, like the left neocortex where our linguistic faculties are located.[15]

There is also an interaction between smell and the sense of touch. Some receptors associated with smell stimulate the trigeminal nerves in the face, which may cause sensations of tingling, temperature change or even pain. We experience these feelings when we smell chemicals like ammonia, menthol and some environmental toxins. At low levels, the feeling may be pleasant; but too much trigeminal stimulation may cause us to back off, perhaps as a survival mechanism.

The complexity of our olfactory receptors and their interactions with odor molecules allows us to differentiate between more than a trillion different scents.[16] What we think of as a single scent is, in fact, a combination of a large number of different odor molecules interacting with a variety of receptors to create an olfactory signature that we then identify as something specific, such as the smell of cinnamon or freshly mown hay.

In spite of this ability to differentiate a huge range of odors, we lack a dedicated olfactory vocabulary that matches the richness of qualitative descriptions we associate with our other senses. This may be related to the olfactory bulb's weak connection to the brain's language center. Rather than describing an odor itself, we usually describe smells by naming the objects that create them. We may say that something smells like a rotten egg or like a lily. Even when we say that something smells sour, this only means that it smells like something that tastes sour. The few words that do directly describe a particular scent are not in common usage. For example, few people know the term "petrichor," which is the earthy scent produced when rain falls on dry soil. Most people are more likely to refer to this odor as "the smell of rain." And although the words for people who cannot see (blind) or hear (deaf) are quite familiar, the word for lacking the sense of smell (anosmia) is recognized only by scientists. Because of this, Diane Ackerman calls smell "the mute sense, the one without words."[17] Scientists still don't agree on the number or types of basic odor classes. Estimates range from between four to nine basic types of smell, and the categories identified frequently follow the familiar habit of naming the cause of the smell, not the smell itself; for instance, "'fruity', 'ethereal', 'burnt', 'waxy' and 'minty.'"[18]

The scientific quantification and qualification of environmental odors—tied closely to the flavors and fragrances industries—has also been relatively slow to emerge. Modern instrumentation, like gas chromatography, provides a molecular fingerprint that identifies odorous chemicals in a laboratory setting. For environmental work, the Nasal Ranger is an "augmented nose" that allows technicians in the field to measure the level of odors.[19] But the evaluation of many scents is still entrusted to trained animals or human specialists, affectionately called "noses."

ATTRACTION, AVERSION, AND IDENTITY

This lack of vocabulary and scientific understanding may reflect smell's reputation as being a "lesser sense" but belies its powerful impact in our lives. Our ability to smell is an integral part of knowing ourselves, our connection with others and our environment. People who have lost their sense of smell report intense feelings of depression and disconnection from the world around them. More than any other sensory experience, odors trigger our deep emotions moving us to tears of joy or rage, plucking our heartstrings or making us cower in fear. The olfactory system's fast track to the brain's emotional center creates intense and immediate reactions to odors—both those we love and those we abhor.

Rather than being genetically encoded with smell preferences, we learn over time to like or dislike specific odors. Rachel Herz, a leading expert on the psychology of smell, notes that infants like the smell of feces and are indifferent to other scents that adults either strongly like or dislike.[20] Since our preferences for odors grow through our experiences and the cultural messages we get, people often disagree on whether a smell is good or bad. I learned this firsthand when a Japanese exchange student offered me a taste of her favorite breakfast of natto, a slimy fermented soybean concoction that some people describe as gaggingly putrid. Usually adventuresome in the food arena, I was barely able to bring the dish to my mouth, let alone taste it. She smiled shyly and told me that, though it's a favorite dish in Japan, many Americans respond this way.

Our evaluation of odors also depends on their location and predictability. As one person on a "smellwalk" (Figure 7.1) through an unfamiliar neighborhood observed,

"you can kind of ignore background smells but then you get arrested by something and there's a really strong detergent smell … that's sort of actually quite offensive … you might find it bearable in a hospital, but anywhere else it's kind of really unpleasant."[21]

Alternately, a "bad" smell in the right location might be a positive addition. For example, the smell of rotting seaweed is not usually one we would like, but when we encounter it at the seashore, it seems appropriate and familiar. We might even miss it if it were absent.

Once an odor is associated with an emotion, future exposure to that odor frequently evokes that same emotion. After dinner at my grandparent's house, my family would often gather in the living room. My grandfather would smoke his evening pipe, and as a child, I'd sit on the floor, lean my head back against his chair and relax

Figure 7.1 These University of Washington students are taking a "smellwalk" around a Seattle neighborhood, recording odors they detect and their reactions to them.

into a dreamy stupor of familiar stories. Now, whenever I encounter the smell of pipe tobacco, a calm settles over me with a sense of protection and well-being. The power of evoked feelings like these add to the effectiveness of aroma-therapies and the commercial power of olfactory branding of products.

THE SMELL OF TIME AND PLACE

On an architectural scale, odors both accompany and create a sense of place. This is true from the macro to the micro scale—the aroma of Tacoma that spreads across miles, the burst of cumin, cardamom and cloves that permeates a Middle Eastern souk, or the faint wisp of cedar clinging to the back of an old closet. The olfactory character of a place reflects a wide range of influences. The local climate and landscape determine an area's flora and fauna, which characterize regional odors like the scent of pine woods or the fragrance of tropical flowers. The temperature, humidity and air movement also contribute. Warmer temperatures increase volatility of molecules and thus enhance odors. Air moisture increases the absorption of odor molecules by the mucous membrane, thus also increasing the intensity of detected odors. Wind and rapid air movement disperse odor molecules, increasing their area of impact but diluting their concentration. All these climatic and geographic differences create a regional olfactory essence that differentiates the basic scent of the eucalyptus groves of northern California from that of a Costa Rican rainforest or the salty brine of the Italian Cinque Terre. To conjure up the atmosphere of exotic places for travelers embarking on a journey, Heathrow airport has even installed a giant, one-of-a-kind "scent globe" which disperses aromas of Thailand (lemongrass, ginger and coconut), Japan (seaweed, green tea and ambergris) and Brazil (coffee, tobacco and jasmine) on command.[22]

Building materials and construction methods add a more fine-grained layer of scent to the built environment. The blend of odors from structural and finish materials and their different absorptive qualities make adobe construction smell different from that of cedar, stone or concrete. Constructed of raw larch and Douglas pine, Peter Zumthor's Swiss Sound Box pavilion at Expo 2000 in Germany permeated the open space with the gentle scent of unfinished wood to evoke the olfactory essence of Swiss forests. Some scents linger for the life of the building. The sandalwood door to the temple of Somnath in India is over 2,000 years old but still emanates its natural scent. Historically, scents were sometimes incorporated into the oils and waxes used to preserve architectural building materials.[23] In contemporary buildings, the odors of synthetic finish materials and furnishings off-gas and contribute their own, sometimes toxic, mix of volatile organic compounds to the olfactory experience.

Industries and activities common to a place also add texture to the smellscape. From the smell of farm animals or industrial processing of paper pulp to the odors of car exhaust fumes and taco stands, human activities have a strong influence on the olfactory character of places. At a smaller scale, the things people gather around them—the detergents and products used to care for or scent the personal environment, and the personal smells we carry on our bodies—all mingle together to create our most intimate smell spaces. Cultures through the ages can be identified by these characteristic odors. The Mesopotamians employed scents of cedar, myrtle and storax. The Egyptians favored incense, myrrh, juniper and sandalwood. The Indians cherished patchouli, incense and vetiver, and the Native Americans, resin and sage.[24]

These smellscapes are sometimes thought of as the olfactory music of place. So it is not surprising that perfumers, the experts in the odor industry, discuss odors in musical terms, recognizing base, middle and top notes of scent. Applying this to the urban smellscape, we can envision a macro-level base note that may be related to the local climate, geography and flora and fauna. The mid-level notes from larger cultural patterns of settlement and industry blend with the background to create an area-based smell. At the micro level, we can detect the high notes of the smellscape—the individual street vendors or strongly scented bushes in bloom—odors that may be intense, changeable and short-lived.[25] In a similar fashion, Malnar and Vodvarka characterize odors that are episodic (foreground or time limited) or background (pervasive or constant).[26]

Whether the composition of all these odors is pleasant or disgusting, sweet or acrid, each one carries an association with a distinct time or place in life, a familiarity that ties us to a shared history. In her pioneering work exploring urban smellscapes, Victoria Henshaw took people on "smellwalks" and created smell maps of neighborhoods around the world to identify their distinctive odors. On one such walk through the summer streets of New York City conducted by Kate Taylor, participants noted that "outside the new Whitney Museum of American Art on Gansevoort Street, the scent of charred meat from the various food stalls blended with the tourists' sunscreens and the salty, muddy smell of the Hudson River."[27]

Often, one smell evolves to another as a person moves through a neighborhood or space. The rhythm of smells may become a signature line for a particular city, neighborhood or season. Pike Place Market in Seattle, for example, is a modulation of smells and sounds (Figures 7.2 and 7.3). Visitors move from the seaside smell and raucous sounds of the fish market to the delicate aroma and relative calm of the flower stalls. A blindfolded person could sense moving in and out of these distinct nodes as if they were separate rooms within the market. Each would be diminished if their wares and sensory cues were intermixed. In a similar fashion, sections of a city have different scent signatures that evolve as one moves from areas dominated by traffic exhaust to ethnic neighborhoods with profusions of traditional cooking odors to a neighborhood park conveying the earthy smells of nature and fresh air (thus sometimes dubbed the "lungs of the city").

Just as odors reveal regional and personal differences, they may also reflect differences through time. Easily changeable, scents may go out of style and come to

Figures 7.2 and 7.3 Seattle's Pike Place Market provides a rich sequence of olfactory experiences as visitors move from the seaside odors of the fish market to the delicate aromas of the flower market.

Olfactory Space

represent an olfactory signature of an era. Few people today can recall the smell of mothballs that heralded the onset of autumn as wool sweaters came out of summer storage in the mid 1900s. The smell of patchouli evokes the 1960s in the United States when a young hippie generation became fascinated with the culture of the Orient. In 2008, architect and preservationist Jorge Otero-Pailos proposed an olfactory reconstruction of three decades in Philip Johnson's Glass House, based on the years 1949, 1959 and 1969. The first fragrance was to recreate the smell of the new house with its blend of newly lacquered wood and painted surfaces, fresh plaster, cement mortar and a hint of leather from the Barcelona chairs. The second would reconstruct a blend of the most popular eau de cologne preferred by sophisticated American men of the mid 1950s. The third was planned to replicate the smell of the house in the late 1960s by which time its porous surfaces had become impregnated with smoke from thousands of cigarettes and cigars.[28] Although this olfactory reconstruction was never approved by the preservationists, it highlights how the evolution of the smellscape can help narrate the history of a place over time.

OLFACTORY POLITICS

The current trend in the design of the built environment is to treat odors as problems and work to eliminate them. In general, we distrust odors. This plays out in common phrases as we say that we "smell a rat" when we are suspicious or that an offer "smells fishy" if it is too good to be true. This distrust was exacerbated during the early Renaissance when the Black Death and other diseases were thought to be transmitted by odors. At this time, towns and cities across Europe were extremely smelly places by today's standards. Burdened with excrement, mud, decomposing animals, vegetables and blood, the urban streetscape was the conduit of noxious odors. This time of living close to the earth and the effluents of human waste was dubbed the "excremental age of architecture" by Barbara and Perliss.[29] Fears of disease generated a movement toward health and sanitation with a focus on the stench, which was alleviated by the use of sweet-smelling herbs and fragrances. During this time, huge quantities of scented "plague water," the precursor to eau de cologne, was sprayed around houses in an attempt to combat the disease.[30]

Industrialization in the early 1800s once again dropped dense urban centers into an olfactory abyss as smokestacks filled the sky with fumes and particulates, byproducts of burning coal in homes and industry. Still believing that disease was carried by foul smells, people feared these rather than the respiratory illness caused by the smoke that accompanied them. Thus began two campaigns to escape the stench. The first was to rid the air of odors with the use of underground sewers and other sanitation works, and the second was to rise above the odors by constructing tall buildings. Dirt and foul scents became associated with lower social class. Sanitization wars were waged as both the home and the city were deodorized or covered over with the smell of scented cleaners and bleach to create an antiseptic aroma of health and acceptability. As the proximity of residential areas to smelly industries began to impact housing prices, zoning codes were introduced, separating residential, commercial and industrial uses. Parks and gardens were popularized for both their open space and clean air.

During the twentieth century, the approach to the olfactory environment was sanitary rather than sensuous. Designers promoted four methods of managing odors in the built environment: separate, dilute, deodorize and mask. The first two of these essentially changed the shape of the smellscape. Separation involved distancing odorous activities and materials away from the areas of human activity or patterns of settlement. Within buildings, smells were segregated to their appropriate rooms and vented directly to the outdoors. To further discourage odors from lingering, furnishings changed from soft and absorbent to hard and impermeable materials. On the urban scale, zoning was enforced and urban traffic patterns were studied to evaluate and reduce growing concerns over pollution levels. The second approach, dilution, was accomplished via naturally and mechanically induced air movement. Stagnant air was the villain. In an attempt to promote air circulation to all housing units, the row house took the place of closed blocks in urban design.[31] Inside buildings, natural and mechanical ventilation was promoted, and national codes were adopted for minimum ventilation standards. The last two odor management methods, deodorization and masking, changed the qualitative experience of the odor in its degree of pleasantness/unpleasantness. Deodorization removed odors through filtration or absorption, while masking covered the undesirable odor with a more desirable scent.

But these improvements in air quality are not equally available to all urban dwellers, raising concerns about health and equity. Since property values are lower near sources of pollution, like industry and traffic, the most devastating impact is the relegation of communities of poverty to these less desirable areas with poorer air quality. Because these communities frequently include recent immigrants from cultures with different olfactory preferences, an extension of this inequality has been to equate culturally unfamiliar odors with poverty and lack of cleanliness. So odor has come to stand as an immediate and emotional social indicator of status, health and safety. Victoria Henshaw observed this on her smellwalks in England when participants reacted to unfamiliar food odors combined with the sounds of different languages and extrapolated these sensory inputs to fears of vulnerability. On noting the smells on a walk through a neighborhood in Doncaster, UK, one participant commented:

> "I don't like Indian food ... It's some foreign foods, the smell that I don't like. ... My partner's father ... a very intelligent, clever man, he wouldn't touch curry ... to save his life, because it's 'foreign muck' ... you're looking at the whole cultural vibration."[32]

Familiar odors associated with wealth, on the other hand, can raise implied social status. On a smellwalk of New York City, master perfumer Céline Barel paused inside the air-conditioned sanctuary of high-end department store Bergdorf Goodman, inhaled and noted: "It smells rich. It's a mix between the wood, the fragrances of the women, the hairspray, the leather. It's opulent."[33]

Since our preferences for scent qualities vary with the individual and the culture, to err on the safe side, it is often said that "the best smell is no smell." Or as Victoria Henshaw put it, "smells are guilty until proven innocent."[34] Unfortunately, as noted in Chapter 1, this politicizing of odors puts us at risk of losing the richness and diversity of our olfactory heritage. In urban neighborhoods, the traditional activities of an area's occupants include associated sensory qualities that imbue that place with a recognizable sensory culture. In deodorizing the environment, authentic engagement with diversity is avoided and our sensory space is flattened. The French movie director Jean Renoir once said, "Wilshire Boulevard. ... It has no smell to it." By this, he meant that in his era, this part of Los Angeles was so culturally homogeneous it lacked character and interest.[35]

An emerging appreciation for the smellscape creates an opportunity to rethink these attitudes. By not addressing odor as simply a problem to be eliminated, design professionals can shape the smellscape to provide both the health of clean, fresh air and the delight of a sensuous olfactory experience. As with the other senses, this exploration starts with an understanding of the shape of olfactory space.

FOLLOW YOUR NOSE

The design of the smellscape involves shaping the volume and location of space the odor occupies as well as its intensity and qualitative characteristics. Approaching olfactory space in this way, we can explore the various shapes of smellscapes in our designs, noting how they can create rooms, corridors, thresholds and plazas of odor and fresh air, just as we have seen with other sensory modes. We can identify smell rooms, like those that have been designed for centuries by landscape architects in the garden environment. For example, the rose garden, popularized in Roman times,[36] is a room defined by scent within the larger garden landscape (Figure 7.4). It is frequently entered through a trellis covered by roses that serves as an olfactory gateway, accentuating the transition from other areas of the garden. Alternately, just as Wright's Usonian houses slid public spaces past each other so that one bled into the next without abrupt separation, the porous olfactory border between building and sidewalk at a café entrance allows odors to escape, blurring the olfactory transition between inside and out.

The qualities of an odor determine whether it becomes a threshold or an obstacle. Our adoption of non-smoking

Figure 7.4 A rose-covered trellis creates an intense threshold of scent for visitors entering the Bagatelle Rose Garden located in the Parc de Bagatelle, Paris.

regulations in buildings sometimes creates olfactory barriers at building entrances when people congregate there for a smoking break. As one person on a smellwalk noted, "I think in the doorways there's quite a problem … it's a bit of a barrier and you have to kind of hold your breath just to go into it … it's not much of an advert just going into a space."[37] The adoption of no-smoking zones directly in front of building entrances alleviates this effect by dispersing smoking activities to other, more distant locations.

The coherence of an olfactory space depends on how steep or gradual the dispersion of odor is. Unlike light rays, smell does not travel in straight lines. Because molecules must be airborne to be sensed, the shape of olfactory space is closely tied to air circulation patterns. Therefore, the pattern of airflow in a building or urban area is a significant factor in shaping olfactory space. Airflow is driven by air pressure differences, with flows moving from areas of high pressure to areas of low pressure. In general, flow is enhanced by high differences in pressure, open pathways, smooth surfaces, and straight or gradually curved passageways. Corners and dead-end corridors trap air and minimize or eliminate flow. In a discussion with scent walk participants, Victoria Henshaw commented:

> "After the walk, we sat in a café, and, over the rich steam of the coffee, reflected on: how the enclosed form of the mixed-use area had helped to ramp-up smell concentration while the long, straight topography of the busy road had promoted wind-flow both diluting and circulating smells around the city; how the waterfront smells had enhanced its soothing qualities and the subtle emanations from the traditional stone of the historic Minster and the surrounding mossy walls added weight to this peaceful ambience; and, how traffic pollutants so dominated the smellscapes near busy roads."[38]

The patterns of flow within a building or through an exterior site can be studied using airflow instruments (anemometers) on-site and/or scale models. Physical model studies are conducted in a wind tunnel or water table where a fluid medium, air or water respectively, flows around a model of the building(s). The resulting current patterns are made visible by use of smoke in the air or dye in the moving water. If the smoke or dye is injected at the site of an olfactory stimulus, these currents show the dispersion of the odor in the space or, from the design perspective, the shape of the olfactory space. Alternately, a computer simulation—for instance, computational fluid dynamics (CFD)—can render the shape of an olfactory space (Figure 7.5). For each of these techniques, the

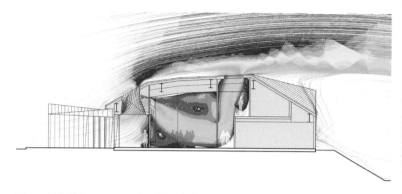

Figure 7.5 This computational fluid dynamics simulation shows the movement of natural ventilation through a building. Color coding indicates areas with high and low ventilation rates.

porousness of the boundary condition (the relative steepness of the olfactory gradient) may be evaluated by the intensity of dispersion of the smoke or dye or a sensitivity analysis in the CFD simulation.

As for the other sensory spaces, the smellscape may also at times be punctuated by an olfactory "event." Smellmarks, analogous to landmarks, highlight a particular aspect of place and orient us in the environment. The scented fountain in Grasse in the south of France is a scentmark for this town, which is known for its perfume industry. A more modest smellmark appears in the courtyard of Asplund's Chapels of Faith and Hope where a scented lavender bush overhanging the walkway creates a burst of scent when visitors brush against it (Figure 7.6).

FROM THE MUNDANE TO THE SUBLIME

As we learn to shape the smellscape, we must also understand the power of the emotional tool we wield. We have already seen the close connection between smell, emotion and memory, and all of these come into play when we choose the shape and qualities of olfactory space. We see this in the use of personal fragrances that linger in

Figure 7.6 Lavender overhanging a walkway near Asplund's Chapels of Faith and Hope creates an olfactory smellmark when someone brushes against it (Erik Gunnar Asplund, Stockholm, 1935–40).

the mind of a lover. But how does this play out in our built environment?

Nowhere is the application of scents more ubiquitous than in the use of patented fragrances in commercial products and retail outlets, sometimes dubbed retail's "fragrant frontier." Commercial entities design and release branded scents to put customers in a spending mood or to engender brand recognition and loyalty, whether to a particular cleaning product or to an entire chain of hotels. Increasingly, airlines, hotels, retail stores, cruise lines and casinos are injecting patented signature scents into air distribution systems in the hope of inducing positive mood states among consumers that may translate into higher sales. Sheraton hotels smell like fig, clove and jasmine;

Westin hotel lobbies favor a white tea scent; while Four Points hotels smell of cinnamon.[39] These hospitality giants may even include those same scents in follow-up mailings to evoke fond vacation memories.

Museums and theme parks also employ crafted scents to enhance their exhibits and attractions. Drawing on the association between urine odors and dark, undesirable places, Thorpe Park in England held a competition in 2010 to find the country's smelliest urine to incorporate into the design of their new horror film-themed attraction.[40]

As scent marketing moves beyond the smell of specific retail articles and extends into the adjacent ambient environment, the legalities of this marketing technique become less clear. Retailers and advertisers sometimes use scent to reach out and occupy space beyond their proscribed footprint. This may have started with the allure of bakeries and sweetshops inadvertently spilling the smells of freshly baked bread and chocolate into adjacent pedestrian areas, but it has led to the intentional broadcasting of enticing aromas to attract the unsuspecting passerby. Today, we encounter convenience stores that pump the smell of coffee out to the gas pumps to increase coffee sales and cookie retailers that broadcast the scent of freshly baked cookies into public areas to increase the effective size of their mall presence. UK pet food maker Wagg Foods even used this approach to reach out to their four-legged customers by creating a series of dog food-scented sidewalk signs to lure pooches and their attending humans. All of these reflect ways to expand the olfactory space and attract the attention (and wallets) of consumers.

Environmental scents are also used to promote physical and psychological health. Potential sources of restorative odors in the urban environment are sometimes grouped into four categories: fresh air (wind and airflow), trees and

Olfactory Space

plantings, water and waterways, and pleasing aromas from nonnatural sources. Although the science behind the exact cause/effect relationship is still evolving, research results support a correlation between specific odors and feelings of calm and well-being. One study demonstrated that 63 percent of patients having an MRI who inhaled a vanilla aroma (and liked it) reported reduced anxiety before the procedure compared to just 4 percent of patients who didn't take in this smell.[41] The ability to reduce anxiety can lead to improvement in other stress-related symptoms. The aromas of basil, thyme, mint, lilac and lavender have been shown to be helpful in reducing headaches and inflammation and in improving sleep, digestion and blood circulation. These positive outcomes have led to the popularity of fragrant herbs and flowers in healing gardens in hospital and nursing home settings.[42]

Our exploration of the power of olfactory space would not be complete without acknowledging its tie to sacred space. Traditionally, scents have been used to evoke spiritual states.[43] From the buhurcu who perfumed sixteenth-century mosques to the sweetgrass smudgings of Native American traditions and the swinging thurible dispensing incense in the Catholic Church, scent has played a central role in places of worship to establish contact with gods and invoke a feeling of reverence. Almost every established religion uses olfactory symbolism to anchor sacred experiences. Sometimes the smoke itself is seen to represent the presence of the deity and, combined with the sweet, musky or acrid smell that accompanies it, transports the faithful to the threshold of the divine.

Whether it causes us to recoil in disgust or transports us to spiritual heights, the olfactory realm pulls at the heartstrings of our memories and emotions. As architects, designers and inhabitants of this volatile realm, we can use its evocative powers to create memorable places that, in turn, call our memories forward.

Notes

1   Mahmoud Darwish, *In the Presence of Absence*, Trans. Sinan Antoon (New York: Archipelago Books, 2011).
2   Timothy Egan, "Tacoma journal; on good days, the smell can hardly be noticed," *The New York Times*, April 3, 1988, www.nytimes.com/1988/04/06/us/tacoma-journal-on-good-days-the-smell-can-hardly-be-noticed.html
3   Jim Torrence and Don Lemon with "Diamond Jim" and the Jazzmasters, *The Aroma of Tacoma*, Panjo Records, February 14, 2015 [video], https://www.youtube.com/watch?v=uw_3aC-avjc
4   Gianni DeMartino, *Odori*, as quoted by Anna Barbara and Anthony Perliss in *Invisible Architecture, Experiencing Places through the Sense of Smell* (Milano: SKIRA Press, 2006), 140.
5   Anthony Synnott, *The Body Social: Symbolism, Self and Society* (London: Routledge, 1993), 183–4.
6   Victoria Henshaw, "Fragrant cities, relationships between smell and environments," cities@manchester blog, March 5, 2012, https://citiesmcr.wordpress.com/2012/03/05/fragrant-cities-relationships-between-smell-and-urban-environments/
7   Victoria Henshaw, "Scents of place: the power of the olfactory," *The Architectural Review*, August 3, 2014, www.architectural-review.com/rethink/scents-of-place-the-power-of-the-olfactory/8666675.fullarticle
8   Avery Gilbert as quoted in Chloe Prasinos, "The sense and sensibility of LA's new nosey perfume enthusiasts," *NPR*, February 22, 2015, www.npr.org/2015/02/22/388245432/the-scents-and-sensibility-of-las-nosy-new-perfume-enthusiasts
9   Ibid.
10 Patrick Süskind as quoted in Ashraf Osman, *Overview of Olfactory Art in the 20th Century*, CAS Seminar Paper (June 24, 2013), https://www.academia.edu/4608919/Historical_Overview_of_Olfactory_Art_in_the_20th_Century_CAS_Seminar_Paper_
11 Henshaw, "Fragrant cities."
12 Anna Barbara and Anthony Perliss, *Invisible Architecture: Experiencing Places through the Sense of Smell* (Milano: SKIRA Press, 2006), 23.
13 Mark Anderson, "Do vibrations help us smell?" *Scientific American*, April 1, 2013, www.scientificamerican.com/article/do-vibrations-help-us-smell/
14 Juhani Pallasmaa, *The Eyes of the Skin: Architecture and the Senses* (West Sussex: John Wiley & Sons, 2005), 54.
15 Barbara and Perliss, *Invisible Architecture*, 111.
16 C. Bushdid, M. O. Magnasco, L. B. Vosshall and A. Keller, "Humans can discriminate more than 1 trillion olfactory stimuli," *Science* 343, no. 6177 (2014), www.sciencemag.org/content/343/6177/1370.full
17 Diane Ackerman, *A Natural History of the Senses* (London: Phoenix, a division of Orion Books Ltd., 2000), 6.
18 Kelvin Low, *Scents and Scent-Sibilities: Smell and Everyday Life Experiences* (Newcastle Upon Tyne: Cambridge Scholars Publishing, 2009), 5.
19 Henshaw, "Fragrant cities."
20 Rachel Herz, *The Scent of Desire: Discovering Our Enigmatic Sense of Smell* (New York: Harper Collins Publishers, 2007), 33.
21 Victoria Henshaw, *Urban Smellscapes* (New York: Routledge, 2014), 152.

22 "Holiday makers 'jet-scent' around the globe," Heathrow press release, http://mediacentre.heathrow.com/pressrelease/details/81/Corporate-operational-24/4334 (accessed October 30, 2014).

23 Barbara and Perliss, *Invisible Architecture*, 65.

24 Ibid.

25 Henshaw, *Urban Smellscapes*, 172.

26 Ibid., 5.

27 Kate Taylor, "The smells of summer," *The New York Times*, NY Region, August 19, 2015, www.nytimes.com/interactive/2015/08/20/nyregion/new-york-city-summer-smells.html

28 Jorge Otero-Pailos, "An olfactory reconstruction of Philip Johnson's Glass House interior," in *After Taste: Expanded Practice in Interior Design*, ed. Kent Kleinman, Joanna Merwood-Salisbury, and Lois Weinthal (New York: Princeton Architectural Press, 2012), 210.

29 Barbara and Perliss, *Invisible Architecture*, 30.

30 Ibid., 171.

31 Ibid., 177.

32 Henshaw, *Urban Smellscapes*, 96–7.

33 Taylor, "The smells of summer."

34 Henshaw, *Urban Smellscapes*, 16.

35 "Films de France," *Le Film Guide*, www.filmsdefrance.com/biography/jean-renoir.html; "Montreal Stinks," *Salbowski: Quite Dashing*, www.salvatoreciolfi.com/?s=Montreal+Stinks (accessed July 20, 2016).

36 "The history of roses," *University of Illinois Extension*, https://extension.illinois.edu/roses/history.cfm (accessed July 20, 2016).

37 Henshaw, *Urban Smellscapes*, 123.

38 Henshaw, "Scents of place."

39 Alun Palmer, "20 fascinating facts about our sense of smell," June 22, 2013, *Mirror*, www.mirror.co.uk/lifestyle/health/20-fascinating-facts-sense-smell-1977351

40 Henshaw, *Urban Smellscapes*, 200.

41 W. H. Redd, S. L. Manne, B. Peters, P. B. Jacobsen, and H. Schmidt, "Fragrance administration to reduce patient anxiety in MRI," *Journal of Magnetic Resonance Imaging* 4, no. 4 (1994), 623–6.

42 Lance Hosey, "Scent and the city," *The New York Times, Sunday Review*, October 25, 2013.

43 Lynne Hume, *Portals: Opening Doorways to Other Realities through the Senses* (Oxford: Berg Publishers, 2007), 109.

Multisensory Design

Chapter 8

"I suppose it's about layering, isn't it? ... layers of senses. If you look at something it might please or displease you on the eye, and then you smell it and that gives you a different level of understanding of whatever you're looking at, and sound is obviously on top of that."[1]

Resident on a smellwalk with Victoria Henshaw in Manchester, UK

Stroll back through the memories of Peter Zumthor and you will find a world alive to the senses. In *Thinking Architecture*, he reminisces about walking into his aunt's house:

> "There was a time when I experienced architecture without thinking about it. Sometimes I can almost feel a particular door handle in my hand, a piece of metal shaped like the back of a spoon. I used to take hold of it when I went into my aunt's garden. That door handle still seems to me like a special sign of entry into a world of different moods and smells. I remember the sound of gravel under my feet, the soft gleam of the waxed oak staircase. I can hear the heavy front door closing behind me as I walk along the dark corridor and enter the kitchen, the only really brightly lit room in the house."[2]

With these words, this master of sensory design lets us sniff and scratch around the world of his youth. He mentions each of the sensory experiences separately, and yet they are part of a unified whole tucked into his memory as his aunt's house, an ordinary and yet delightfully unique place in the world for him.

We have explored the individual senses and noted how their physical shapes hover as invisible spaces to inhabit—rooms, alcoves and thresholds in the environment around us. In this chapter, we will turn our attention to the interaction among the senses, noting what happens as they overlap each other and the corresponding tectonic space. We'll note how they progress rhythmically or haphazardly, work together to build to an intensity, or contradict each other to create an illusion.

We have investigated the sensory world one sense at a time, but there is only one unified world that we experience. As Blesser and Salter point out,

"Although, normally, each of us can fuse any combination of aural, visual, tactile and olfactory inputs into a cognitive map, it is only a single mental map because there is only one single external reality. For example, when touching, hearing, and seeing a violin, there is still only one violin, not separate visual, aural, and tactile violins. The same principle applies to space: different senses provide access to different aspects of a single space. Vision is better for sensing an object's distance; hearing is better for sensing the volume of an enclosed space; and touch is better for sensing surface texture. ... We combine sensory cues and then interpret them using our memory of previous experiences to create a compelling internal sense of an external world. ... There is increasing evidence that cognitive maps of space have dedicated neurological substrates that combine visual and auditory input. These substrates contain a fused representation of spatial attributes. ... When multisensory inputs are aligned, we experience a single object with aural and visual properties; you do not experience an aural object and a visual object."[3]

On the other hand, when sensory attributes are not synchronized, as when the recorded sound in a movie does not match the speaker's lip movement, then we differentiate two separate sensory inputs. So our experience of these sensory realms depends on how they overlap and reinforce each other.

One of the fascinating aspects of their overlap is the transference that sometimes happens from one sense to another. In an extreme form of this, when one sense is stimulated, another also responds. In *The Man Who Tasted Shapes*, Richard Cytowic describes meeting Michael Watson at a dinner party. Agonizing over a chicken he had prepared for the dinner, Michael said that it felt too round, almost spherical, when he had wanted it to feel more spiky.[4] Michael, who perceives taste and smell as physical touch sensations, experiences synesthesia, a phenomenon named from the ancient Greek words *syn* (together) and *aisthēsis* (sensation) in which stimulation of one sensory pathway leads to involuntary experiences in a second. Another way this sensory mixing may occur is for people to see colors when they hear particular sounds. Or sometimes, black letters printed on white paper may each appear in a different specific color. Synesthetes may even learn to spell by recognizing the sequence of colors of letters in a word. Other people physically experience touch when they see someone else being stroked or punched. This is called mirror-touch synesthesia and may be related to the experience of empathy.[5] These occurrences are rare, but they serve to illuminate the ways in which we combine sensory information to comprehend our world.

Although most of us don't have these extreme synesthetic experiences, we all exhibit some tendencies toward it, like associating low musical notes with darker colors and higher notes with bright colors. Our language is full of cross-references like the "warmth" of a shade of red or a "cold" grey tone. We may remark that a rose "whispers" its scent or say that some smells are "sharp," some tastes are "smooth," some sounds are "soft," and others "jar" us. Many times these associations are strengthened by sensory experiences that are coupled in our memory; others indicate the extent to which the sensory experience grabs our attention or affects us emotionally. For example, we say that bold colors *shout* their presence, meaning that our reaction is the same as if we had heard a loud noise.

To understand how sensory experiences overlap in the built environment, sensory researchers develop schematic notations to record sensory phenomena across space and time. In her pioneering smellwalk work, Victoria Henshaw and her coworkers used notations on a map or plan of the site, some of which are animated to show how odors migrate over time. Some evaluation schemes use a polarity of qualities for each sensory input. For example, thermal input may be judged on a scale from hot to cold and kinesthetic space on a range from fluid to constrained. A building or room or outside area can be rated based on these scales. Malnar and Vodvarka developed a set of sensory "sliders" that record sensory experiences at a particular location and time.[6] Valerie Mace adapted their approach to create the sensory flow diagram, as illustrated in Figure 8.1. This diagram compares the experience in five urban outdoor areas (exterior "rooms") in central London.[7] It reveals that while the touch qualities are similar for all of the areas, some are noisy while others are quiet, and that although all of them tend to be kinesthetically constrained, they vary as to how much.

The work of Lucas and Romice takes this a step further by developing a vocabulary of words (qualitative descriptors) to accompany a sensory notation scheme that is charted on a radar-like series of concentric circles (Figure 8.2). Each radial spoke represents a different sensory mode. The distance from the center of the circle

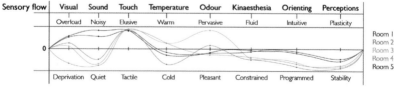

Figure 8.1 This sensory flow diagram by Valerie Mace maps and compares the sensory characteristics of five outdoor "rooms" in central London. This approach is adapted from the sensory slider diagrams created by Malnar and Vodvarka.

Multisensory Design

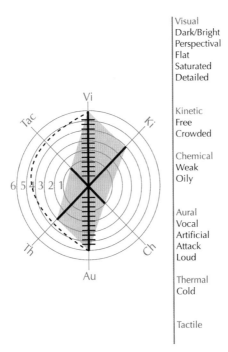

Visual
Dark/Bright
Perspectival
Flat
Saturated
Detailed

Kinetic
Free
Crowded

Chemical
Weak
Oily

Aural
Vocal
Artificial
Attack
Loud

Thermal
Cold

Tactile

Figure 8.2 This sensory notation scheme by Lucas and Romice is charted on a series of concentric circles. Each radial spoke shows a distinct sensory mode, and its distance from the center represents the intensity of the sensory experience. The radial axis is coded to reflect the spatial and temporal qualities, and a dashed line is added to indicate linked sensory experiences.

represents the strength of the sensory experience. The radial axis is also coded to reflect the spatial and temporal qualities of the experience (singular, constant, directional, repetitive, etc.), and a dashed line is added to indicate linked sensory experiences. The relevant qualitative descriptors are listed at the side of the chart.[8] These diagrams are sometimes accompanied by a 500–1,000-word narrative of the sensescape. Raymond Lucas has produced the *Sensory Notation Handbook* to provide training in the use of this recording technique.[9]

All of these schematic frameworks help to evolve a language to describe and record the experiential characteristics of diverse sensory environments. But as we have discovered again and again in our exploration of the senses, there is no substitute for directly experiencing how the senses play off each other in a particular place and time. We can explore these overlaps at two extremes— when they harmonize and reinforce each other to create strong sensory nodes or, alternately, when they contrast with dissonance to create sensory illusions.

HARMONY

When complementary sensory experiences are coupled, their effect increases, like two additive waves, and strengthens the sensory node. Lawrence Hass notes this effect in his discussion on the philosophy of Merleau-Ponty:

> "In virtually every experience of things in the world, there is an overlapping of at least some of our sense modalities, just as there is an overlapping of views in binocular vision. And just as binocular vision yields an experience of the world's depth, the overlapping of sense modalities gives the things we perceive depth, consistency and density."[10]

The sensory node created by this overlap is differentiated from a background with contrasting characteristics and is intensified if the boundary conditions change rapidly (i.e. have a steep gradient). For example, an inglenook is a small kinesthetically confined alcove off a larger room. The inglenook's sensory experience is intensified by overlaps of the warm thermal space of the fire, the flickering orange light space of the flames, the crackling sound space and the smoky olfactory space. The alcove's shape and size intensifies the sensory experiences within it and creates a sharp gradient of change at its edge, providing a strong contrast with the larger, cooler adjacent space.

Some forms encourage or discourage these overlaps. Inside corners tend to shun light and air movement. We know this from wind tunnel studies and from how dust bunnies hide in them. Shadows cling to corners while rounded surfaces yield gently, gradually to shadow. Corners may also shun or distort sound. Windows, on the other hand, couple light and thermal properties. Our nostalgia for window seats speaks to this nodal experience. In sunny weather, windows let in large amounts of both daylight and heat, creating a memorably cheery, warm alcove. But when the sky is overcast, they can be a source of drab light and cold if the window is not well insulated. So the experience of this sensory node depends on the orientation of the window, the weather and climate, and the thermal characteristics of the glazing assembly. For this reason, many historic window seats came equipped with dense thermal curtains to close them off in winter.

Using passive solar strategies, designers can create these nodal sensory experiences throughout a building, landscape or urban area by modulating all of the sensory dimensions to reinforce the public or private nature of a gathering place or refuge. By adding active control of electric lighting, mechanical heating/cooling systems, audio amplification, etc., designers can further sculpt the sensory layers.

DISSONANCE

The opposite interaction happens when the information from two or more senses conflicts. This mismatch creates confusion or illusion. Our brains naturally combine and compare information from multiple senses to create a holistic understanding of the world. Unintentional conflict can cause disharmony and confusion; intentional and meaningful conflict will create energetic tension or illusion.

In the architectural classic *Body, Memory, and Architecture*, Bloomer and Moore acknowledge that "the meanings we assign to buildings are first known haptically, and visual messages in the design signal and recall more fundamental haptic properties by *illuminating or disguising* a building's invitations, dangers and complexities"[11] (italics added). Evaluating the power in Bernini's forecourt for St. Peter's in Rome, they point out that this

> "is an extraordinarily sophisticated example of visual cues (given by the receding side colonnades and by the statues, which are larger near the façade of the cathedral than near the main elliptical space) counterpointing haptic cues (which reveal how far away the façade is). This is much more than a perspectival trick to make the façade seem closer; it pits one sense against another for a powerfully unsettling experience."[12]

Professor Galen Minah, an expert on color and architectural form, explores the potential of color space to distort perceived form in the Color and Light class he teaches at the University of Washington. In this class, students create illusory visual forms by applying color swatches to two cubes that touch at only one edge (Figures 8.3–8.5). Their assignment is to use the advancing and receding characteristics of colors to create an illusion of form that does not exist in the haptic world. These illusive spaces can only be viewed from one angle and collapse into chaos when viewed at other angles.

This exercise with two small blocks can be scaled up to our built environment. For example, we hold many expectations about how surfaces relate to pattern. We expect lines to remain straight, so when they bend and

Figures 8.3–8.5 This student project from Professor Galen Minah's Color and Light class at the University of Washington illustrates how the advancing and receding characteristics of colors and color constancy can create an illusion of form that does not exist in the haptic world. Students apply color swatches to two cubes that touch at only one edge. The top image shows the illusion of L-shaped walls bracketing a smaller cube which projects forward; the middle image shows how the illusion collapses when viewed from a different angle; the bottom image shows the base form of the two actual cubes.

contort, we take that as a signal about the surface they appear on. However, the space that our muscles experience may be different from what our eyes prepare us for. Our muscles communicate the push and pull of our body against the surfaces of a space. When visual signals give us conflicting information (or no information, as in a whiteout when we are skiing), we may stumble or fall. For example, the mind-bending carpet pattern in Figure 8.6 makes the flat floor appear to undulate beneath the feet, energizing the space by creating a sense of tension and instability. More subtle applications of illusion occur when we use dropped lighting in a tall space to reduce its apparent height or when we use mirrored reflections to extend a tight space or to visually hide it.

Figure 8.6 A patterned carpet by EGE Atelier creates the convincing illusion of a warped floor plane, adding a sense of instability and excitement to this video game store in Paris.

Multisensory Design

Whether reinforced with harmony or contrasted with illusion, the integrated experience of a place is more than the sum of its individual layered sensory inputs. As Steven Holl points out in his chapter in *Questions of Perception*,

> "While a cinematic experience of a stone cathedral might draw the observer through and above it … only the architecture itself offers the tactile sensations of textured stone surfaces and polished wooden pews, the experience of light changing with movement, the smell and resonant sounds of space, the bodily relations of scale and proportion. All these sensations combine within one complex experience, which becomes articulate and specific, though wordless. The building speaks through the silence of perceptual phenomena."[13]

The following sections explore memorable works of architecture that probe this depth of multisensory experience. Although, as Holl acknowledges, words cannot capture the entirety of the experience, perhaps they will evoke the spirit of these special places.

PLAY THIS HOUSE LIKE AN INSTRUMENT: ACID MODERNISM (DOUG AITKEN WORKSHOP, 2012)

What if, rather than an engineered machine for living, a house were a sensory art space full of possibilities, fluid and changeable with the people who occupy it and the forces of nature touching upon it (Figure 8.7). This might be the description for the house Doug Aitken, an internationally acclaimed multimedia artist, designed for himself in Venice, California. Aitken's art fuses photography, video, film, words, images, nature and live performance into engaging multimedia experiences. Never singly focused, his works are a communication with the viewer/ occupant, celebrating both change and connection. They engage us, make us consider, question, interact and have

Figure 8.7 American artist and filmmaker Doug Aitken created a multisensory house that combines interactive elements, including a musical table (foreground) and stairs, and illusions, like the silkscreened walls that disappear into the exterior foliage in the right lighting conditions.

our own experience. As he blurs the line between life and art, it should be no surprise that the house he designed for himself is a multisensory living experience that merges the firmness of shelter with the delight of play. In a style he calls "Acid Modernism,"[14] Aitken both combines sensory spaces to create intense multisensory experiences and contrasts them to create illusions.

Concealed by foliage and a surrounding partition, the house itself disappears into the landscape until you pass through a gate at which point the front door suddenly appears before you. Just as the exterior shrinks into the landscape, the interior expands into it, a "liquid architecture" of space not bound to form.[15] Interior living area walls are silkscreened to simulate the hedges growing outside the windows, and in the right light, the solid walls

Multisensory Design

dissolve into the surrounding landscape, turning the space inside out.

Topped by a large skylight, an open stairwell forms the nodal center of the house, a glowing light space amplified by mirrors that line its walls. But it's not a calm, static space. The angled mirrors dance with reflections creating a kaleidoscopic, almost hallucinogenic event. The reflections of a single person walking up the stairs create diminishing images of dozens of clones receding into the depths of a virtual space. At the top, a mirrored sky wraps down into the stairwell itself, again blurring inside and out.

Strengthening this sensory node, the stairs themselves are tuned with a half dozen microphones that turn footsteps into a rhythmic percussion of ascending tones, heightening awareness of the body's movement as it ascends and descends. But the musical stairway also creates a reason to pause. For those who have more time to play, Aitken keeps some lightweight mallets available for more prolonged musical performances on the steps.

The rooms of the house cluster around this central light/sound/haptic node with their own playful sensory effects. Sound is a common theme as Aitken uses it to create links between the physical space and the materiality of the surrounding environment. To pick up the tick and groan of tectonic plate movements from deep inside the Earth, he embedded nine accelerometers and geologically sensitive microphones in the house foundation walls. Also capturing the grumble of tides and drone of traffic, these patient sentinels are connected to speakers throughout the house that Aitken can tune in to at the turn of a dial.[16] This sound space connects the house interior with roots deep inside the Earth.

Other playful soundmarks enliven and create the collaborative, experiential space Aiken desired for his residence. For example, two large tables in the house are functional dining areas as well as being musical instruments. One, shown in Figure 8.7, is a hollow wooden structure with tuned openings, and the other is composed of suspended marble and stone tiles. Each can be played like a xylophone.

In both his art and his home, Doug Aitken transforms the viewer/occupant into a fully immersed participant in a shimmering, illusory world of vanishing boundaries, fractured space and clandestine passages.[17] His design both moves you out of reality and solidly grounds you within it with touchstones to the movement of time and light and the deep growl of the Earth itself.

SEVEN BOTTLES OF LIGHT IN A STONE BOX: CHAPEL OF ST. IGNATIUS (STEVEN HOLL ARCHITECTS, 1997)

On a more contemplative note, Steven Holl's Chapel of St. Ignatius at Seattle University shines as a sacred beacon in a relatively secular city. The Pacific Northwest is sometimes called the "none zone" because of the number of people who claim no religious affiliation, but there is still an affinity for the sacred that resonates with this tiny Jesuit chapel. Perhaps it is the call to the senses that speaks to each of us regardless of our spiritual leanings.

The chapel is in some ways a collaboration between two phenomenologists across four centuries. Drawing on inspiration from the sixteenth-century writings of St. Ignatius, Holl noted that

> "St. Ignatius of Loyola's *The Spiritual Exercises*, printed in 1548, argued for a philosophical interpretation of the senses. This work, preceding later writings on phenomenology by three hundred years, reorders the hierarchy of the five senses. Hearing becomes the most

refined sense while sight—the traditionally dominant sense—comes third after touch. The phenomenal teachings of St. Ignatius became a primary source of inspiration as Tim Bade and I studied and worked on the design."[18]

A master in expressing the materiality of light, Holl used the concept of seven bottles of light arising within in a stone box for the overall form of the chapel (Figure 8.8). Light passing through each "bottle" creates a pool of clear or colored light that delineates a physical space within the chapel and highlights one aspect of Catholic worship. The seven bottles correspond to the entry, narthex, nave, Reconciliation Chapel, choir, Chapel of the Blessed

Figure 8.8 The Chapel of St. Ignatius (Steven Holl Architects, Seattle, 1997) was designed around the concept of seven bottles of light arising within a stone box. Each "bottle" is defined by a colored lens and complementary reflective field, which is accomplished by baffles that are back-painted and illuminated by either daylight or electric light. This image of the east wall of the nave shows its blue lens and yellow reflected field.

Sacrament and bell tower. Each of these light volumes pairs a lens in a pure color with a contrasting field of a reflected complementary color. The high clerestory opening in the choir combines a red lens with a green reflected color field. The nave creates a gradient in color fields that moves from a blue lens and yellow reflected field on the east to a yellow lens with blue reflected field toward the west. The reflected colors are accomplished by baffles that are back-painted and illuminated by either daylight or electric light. Thus the congregation sees only a glow of color seeping out from around the baffle and shimmering upon the wall surrounding the lens of complementary color. The tension between these contrasting colors creates vibrancy at their edges. This is especially noticeable where the lens is within the congregant's normal field of vision above the altar. During the day, the colored light varies with the sky conditions. When the sun peeks out from behind a cloud, a pulse of reflected color enlivens the contemplative space below. At night, these light volumes reach outward as beacons across the campus and into the adjacent neighborhood.

Generally, the electric lights are hidden behind the baffles. In the nave, however, pendant lighting in an irregular grid of hand-blown dropped "stars" generates a mid-height play of brilliants that enliven the space and capture an intermediate, human-scaled volume beneath the soaring space above.

The chapel's representation of "a gathering of different lights" is an apt metaphor for Seattle University's mission to serve many nationalities of students. It also refers to St. Ignatius' vision of the spiritual life as comprising many interior lights and darknesses that he called "consolations" and "desolations," all of which he understood as contributing to growth along a spiritual path.[19]

Although light was the generating concept, the sense of touch is the first to greet visitors to the building. Wide doors of Alaskan cedar reflect southern sunlight from the facets of hand-hewn texture reminiscent of fish scales that dimple their surface. The over-wide Alaskan cedar doors, one smaller than the other, symbolize the traditional practice of a tall ceremonial entry and a lower private one. The thickness of the doors is exaggerated by lensed ellipses that cut through the cedar on an angle to splash ovals of sunlight on the interior floor. The gracefully curving ribbon of brass in the door handles welcomes the hand's touch. Two contrasting haptic messages of substance and ease are combined in these oversized doors, which seem to glide open with surprisingly little effort for their thickness and weight.

Stepping inside, the visitor is swept forward on a polished black concrete floor that mimics the surface of the reflecting pool outside and guides flow through the building, ramping gradually up from the entry to the sanctuary. The narthex opens off to the right of this ramp like an eddy pool off the main flow. Here, a large island of thick handwoven wool rug invites people to gather. Throughout the building, wall surfaces are covered with hand-scratched plaster in a rectangular patchwork pattern. The play of light across this surface causes the texture to pop to life or disappear depending on the light's angle of incidence. Heavy in texture when grazed by light, the surface flattens and dematerializes as the sky becomes overcast.

The sense of hearing, which St. Ignatius considered the most refined sense, has also received careful attention. By focusing the radial point of the curved roofs either above the human ear or below the level of the floor, the acoustics of the sanctuary are skillfully shaped for both chamber and vocal music.[20] The resulting sound fills the space without hot spots or confusing echoes. Although an amplifying system was installed in the building, it is rarely used because the acoustics are excellent without it.

A quietly surprising sensory space in the building is the Chapel of the Blessed Sacrament (Figures 8.9 and 8.10). Terminating the view from the entry processional, this tiny chapel is focused on a honey onyx tabernacle lit from within. Arching above this is the graceful silhouette of a madroña tree from which hangs a delicate lantern of amber cast glass. The entire room exudes a soft red-orange glow, the sixth of Holl's seven bottles. Stepping into the chapel on a warm summer day, visitors enter a sacred olfactory space laden

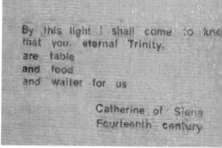

By this light I shall come to know
that you, eternal Trinity,
are table
and food
and waiter for us

Catherine of Siena
Fourteenth century

Figures 8.9 and 8.10 Walls in the tiny Chapel of the Blessed Sacrament at the Chapel of St. Ignatius are coated with beeswax that creates a sweet aroma in summer months when sunlight warms the room. Religious quotes beneath the beeswax layer entice visitors to come close to the walls where the scent is strongest (Steven Holl Architects, Seattle, 1997; artist: Linda Beaumont).

with the sweet aroma of beeswax. This atmosphere is the work of local artist Linda Beaumont who inlaid prayers into the plaster walls before coating them with translucent beeswax. As summer sun heats up the space, the wax gives off a faint scent that intensifies as visitors lean in toward the wall to read the prayers. As Linda notes, "the scent recalls the ancient church, the room becomes a candle."[21] And visitors take their place within the flame of this olfactory alcove.

WARMTH BORN OF THE MOUNTAIN DEPTH: THERME VALS (PETER ZUMTHOR, 1996)

Mention sensory space among a group of architects and Peter Zumthor's name is sure to come up. He is well known now but that was not yet the case when he designed what has been called a timeless piece of architecture and one of the most iconic works in contemporary Swiss design— Therme Vals.[22]

On a southeast-facing hillside of the narrow Vals valley in the eastern Swiss Alps, the project site is home to mountain vistas and a natural thermal spring. Spring water, rich in therapeutic minerals, flows from the ground at a comfortable temperature of 86°F (30°C). Some data suggest that use of the springs here dates back to the Bronze Age, but their recent development as a destination resort occurred in the 1960s when a hotel complex was developed to replace the earlier nineteenth-century therapeutic baths. When this new facility fell on hard times in the mid 1980s, the municipality took it over and held a design competition for a new spa facility. Peter Zumthor won the competition.[23]

His sensitive design for the spa has been well reported elsewhere. So, here, we will explore the sequence of sensory experiences it creates rather than dwell on the architectonic construction itself. Preserving views from the existing hotel, Zumthor's spa building is bermed deep into the hillside, rotated about 30 degrees relative to cardinal directions. Its southeast and southwest elevations emerge from the slope and open to the light. Constructed of 60,000 slabs of the local Valser gneiss stone,[24] the building seems less like a construction and more a recess carved into the mountain itself. Sensuous volumes of water, heat, light, sound and aroma hover within this angular quartzite enclosure. The stone, solid and timeless, both grounds and contrasts the mutable and ephemeral sensory spaces it contains.

Descending from the hotel, visitors follow a curving subterranean tunnel through the bowels of the mountain to access the spa. This primordial entry sequence serves to disconnect the spa from the stress and activities of daily life on the Earth's surface. At the spa level, the entry continues its mystery with a labyrinthian path that leads through a turnstile and changing rooms and provides fleeting glimpses into the larger space and to the valley beyond. Visitors may hear water running over stone and the distant echo of laughter but not see their sources.

Within the main spa room, daylight streaming through gaps in the ceiling joints grazes the stacked stone slabs, exaggerating their texture (Figure 8.11). Their massive weight lends a sense of refuge. Also, the primary materials in the spa—stone, concrete, glass and water—offer little sound absorption, creating a relatively alive acoustic space. In the bathing areas, the combination of the large acoustic horizons and the quiet solemnity of the stone tectonic encourages whispered communications. Here, private acoustic arenas are held close to the body, regulated by volume of voice and turn of the head, and often extend less than an arm's length from the parties involved in conversation.

Figure 8.11 Therme Vals' main interior pool is lit by blue skylights and slits of daylight at roof joints (Peter Zumthor, 1996).

This is an underground sensory world of modern spaces celebrating the primal ritual of bathing. The rough texture of the stone walls contrasts with the velvet surface of the water, sleek glass windows and polished brass handrails. Only in areas of the building designed for private use, such as the changing rooms and therapy rooms, are the vertical surfaces polished and refined.

Light levels inside the building are kept intentionally low, accentuating information from other senses. The relative darkness of the walls absorbs much of the incident light and makes the light space appear to hover and glow around its sources, whether from daylight or electric light fixtures. The small pendant electric lights suspended in the space are floating points of light quickly swallowed up by the surfaces around them. When illumination comes from above the pools, the stone below water level may appear dark and viscous like a pool in a stone quarry. But when the pools are lit from below, they become watery volumes of light that extend upward into the vapors rising from their surface.

A natural progression of thermal spaces leads from the warmer sections of the building that are bermed into the hill to the cooler areas that project out from it, and the locations of most of the pools reflect this natural gradient. The large central interior pool is kept slightly below skin temperature and shimmers in cool blue light emanating from a grid of blue glazed skylights above and the water below. Other smaller pools and thermal alcoves scattered around this larger bathing area are hidden from view by the stone monoliths that enclose them. Pools of light lead the visitor on a meandering path of discovery from one sensory space to the next. Warmer pools, like the Fire Bath at 107°F (42°C),[25] glow in red tones, and cold baths have a blueish tint that reinforces their thermal experiences. The scent of flower petals floating in the Flower Bath creates a cloud of perfumed air above its surface. And everywhere the faint scent (and perhaps even taste) of minerals in the air pervades the space.

Zumthor also gifts spa visitors with unique sound experiences. One, the Sound Bath (sometimes called the resonance room), is a narrow, tall space with rough-faced stone that creates echoing reverberations, encouraging visitors to hum or sing. Another, the Sounding Stone, is a passive space where visitors lounge on sculpted leather recliners and are immersed in the recorded percussive music of stones hitting against each other as composed by Fritz Hauser. Each of these creates a mesmerizing alcove of sound space within the greater volume of the spa.

Transitioning to the outdoor pool, bathers move from a place of refuge to one of prospect with views opening to

Figure 8.12
At night when the outdoor pool is lit from below, it becomes a watery volume of light that extends upward into the vapors rising from its surface (Peter Zumthor, 1996).

the valley. Here, the light space widens to include the sky. This expanse of light and the splash of brisk mountain air contrasts with the closeness and humidity of interior spaces. The temperature of the exterior pool is changed seasonally. In summer, it is close to the temperature of the interior pool. In winter, it is raised to 97°F (36°C) to make bathers more comfortable in the chilly air (Figure 8.12). The sensory space around this pool also changes at night when the light from the pool rises with the steam, becoming a "territory of light and warmth beneath the dark and cold of the sky."[26] This magical realm is reinforced by the change in the acoustic space as water jets are silenced and bathers quiet their conversations in response. In this way, the outdoor pool is transformed from a transparent and unbounded sensory space during the day to an intimate bubble of vaporous light and hushed voices at night.

Therme Vals was named a National Monument just two years after its completion in 1996. Zumthor has said of Vals that it "is not about an outside object. … It is about what happens inside, the bathing oriented toward the ritual as if in the Orient. It's about water and stone and light and sound and shadow."[27] The sensory spaces he has created here are a testament to that. The exquisite union of both the visible and invisible architecture at Therme Vals makes it float in the memory long after one has left the site.

VOICE OF THE SEA; LIGHT OF THE SUN: SEA ORGAN (NIKOLA BAŠIĆ, 2005) AND GREETING TO THE SUN (NIKOLA BAŠIĆ, 2008)

Stripped down to the bare form of sound and light—no walls or roof, no doors or windows—Nikola Bašić's Sea Organ and Greeting to the Sun, situated in Zadar, Croatia, alongside one another, are constructions of the senses alone (Figure 8.13). Though frequently described as ephemeral, they are also as substantial as the Roman

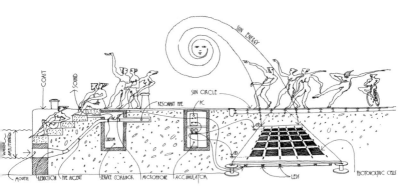

Figure 8.13 Nikola Bašić's sketch of the Marinaprojekt (2005, 2008) illustrates how wave action activates sonic chambers within the Sea Organ and solar radiation charges the light space of Greeting to the Sun.

ruins and medieval churches scattered around Zadar and, perhaps, visited more often. You're sure to find them named among Croatia's top tourist attractions, but they offer not just a place to be viewed, photographed and checked off a list of tourist sites. Rather, this is a place to inhabit, linger and be held within the ancient song of the sea and the dancing lights of a more modern world.

Situated on the western coast of a peninsula that juts out into the azure Adriatic, Zadar is a quintessential Roman city. During most of its history, Zadar was huddled inside ancient walls, protected from the adjacent sea whose myriad islands gave harbor to potential invaders. Thus to local residents, the sea beyond the walls represented a source of both joy and fear, a place of expansive horizons and glorious sunsets as well as lurking dangers.[28] During World War II, however, the danger descended from the sky as Zadar endured heavy bombing that destroyed 60 percent of its buildings. Reconstruction after the war turned much of the waterfront into an unbroken, monotonous concrete wall.[29] Decayed and neglected, this grey wasteland became a "paradox of periphery in the city centre."[30] Its natural beauty went largely unappreciated.

Local residents refer to the old town section of Zadar as "the stone ship" because of its position on the narrow peninsula. In 2004, the local port authority decided to reconstruct the "prow" of the peninsula to enable passing cruisers to dock. Drawing on childhood experiences of sailing up this coastline on a small single-masted fishing boat with his father, Bašić's design for this dynamic place where water meets land creates two experiential places, a sound space and a light space, that magically connect the natural and the urban.

In writing about the first of these, Bašić observes:

> "I became aware that on the global line dividing the two media, the sea and the land, the one that shapes the islands and the continents, the clash of these two media had always been resolved by sound. How much this inevitable encounter could be poetic but also dramatic was close to me because of my childhood spent on an island. I was aware that sound gives an additional dimension to every coastal space, a dimension of the spatial sound or the acoustic space."[31]

Bašić's Sea Organ gives a musical voice to this acoustic dimension (Figure 8.14). It uses the power of the waves to force air through a series of underwater pipes embedded in a wide marble stairway that lines the water's edge. Heaving seawater enters the immersed tubes and works like a piston to push air through a resonant chamber under the promenade. The musical tones created in this way exit through openings at the top of the stairs. Altogether, the Sea Organ has 35 pipes in sets of five, spread across seven segments of stone steps. The sets of pipes are tuned to one of two major chords that span a masculine vocal range, similar to that found in traditional Dalmatian songs. In

Figure 8.14 At the Sea Organ, a series of underwater pipes embedded in the stairs creates sonic chambers that use wave action to generate hypnotic melodies. The stairs are a popular gathering place for tourists and locals (Nikola Bašić, Marinaprojekt d.o.o., 2005).

this way, musically coherent harmonies are created out of randomly generated wave energies. The resulting hypnotic melody sounds, at times, like the light dance of panpipes and, at other times, like the melancholic call of a deep-sea creature. The music varies depending on the weather, the tides and currents, and the wakes of passing boats.[32]

In contrast to the Sea Organ, which uses techniques from antiquity, Greeting to the Sun is a sophisticated light show that could only be achieved with modern technology (Figure 8.15). It is a large disc, 72 ft (22 m) in diameter, embedded in the surface of the promenade at the tip of the peninsula. A narrow metal band inscribed with saints' days from ancient Zadar and other astronomical data separates the disc from the surrounding pavement. Within the disc are a series of solar cells that power 10,000 LED lights

Figure 8.15 At night, Greeting to the Sun creates a dramatic light space with patterns timed to sounds emanating from the Sea Organ (Nikola Bašić, Marinaprojekt d.o.o., 2008).

spread across the disc's surface. Each LED lamp changes intensity and color based on computer input correlated with the tones from the Sea Organ, thus producing a coordinated sound and light experience. The perceived light intensity increases as daylight diminishes. But this is not a light show to be observed from afar. The installation has a walkable surface that entices visitors to dance or stroll or watch the sunset while engulfed within its dynamic sensory space (Figure 8.16). The installation may even be programmed to respond to movement on its surface, establishing an interactive communication between the visitors and the light around them.

The Sea Organ and Greeting to the Sun connect people and nature, land and sea, modernity and antiquity. They move the focus from the materially solid, orderly, Roman built environment of reason and logic to the mystical,

Multisensory Design

Figure 8.16 At Greeting to the Sun, women dance in celebration of the sunset (Nikola Bašić, Marinaprojekt d.o.o., 2008).

ephemeral space of the senses.[33] The sound space of the Sea Organ encompasses a larger area and has boundaries more porous than those of the light space. Approaching the site, the visitor enters the sound space as a gradual gradient, first tentatively, as a distant whisper, then building in intensity. The light space is embedded within the sound space and is more confined with sharper boundaries.

A photograph can't capture the essence of this immaterial architecture, but it can capture its effect on the people gathered there. Without the people, there's not much to note in these simple elements—a series of sleek white marble steps leading to the sea, a large glossy circle within the ground plane. Yet the magical presence of place cannot be denied. If it is true that the use of a place is judged by what is left behind, then the discards here have a passionate story to tell. When the local diving club was tasked with cleaning the sea bottom in front of the Sea Organ, rather than the expected litter of empty beer cans and candy wrappers, they found women's and men's underwear![34] Whether a place of passionate lovers, playing children or contemplative meditators, Bašić's creation at the water's edge is ever-changing, evolving with the volatile temperament of the sea and the predictable logic of a computer program. Yet it is also perpetually present, gathering people together within an architecture of the senses.

Notes

1   Victoria Henshaw, *Urban Smellscapes: Understanding and Designing City Smell Environments* (New York: Routledge, 2014), 75.
2   Peter Zumthor, *Thinking Architecture*, 3rd Edition (Basel: Birkhauser, 2010), 7.
3   Barry Blesser and Linda-Ruth Salter, *Spaces Speak, Are You Listening?* (Cambridge: The MIT Press, 2009), 47.
4   Richard E. Cytowic, *The Man Who Tasted Shapes* (Cambridge: The MIT Press, 2003), 4.
5   Michael J. Banissy and Jamie Ward, "Mirror-touch synesthesia is linked with empathy," *Nature Neuroscience*, June 17, 2007, www.daysyn.com/Banissy_Wardpublished.pdf
6   Joy Monice Malnar and Frank Vodvarka, *Sensory Design* (Minneapolis: University of Minnesota Press, 2004), 247–51.
7   Valerie Mace, "Sensing the urban interior," Plenary Session, *[in]arch International Conference*, Java, Indonesia, September 10–11, 2014, https://www.academia.edu/8379344/Sensing_the_Urban_Interior
8   Raymond Lucas and Ombretta Romice, "Assessing the multi-sensory qualities of urban space: a methodological approach and notational system for recording and designing the multi-sensory experience of urban space," *Psychology* 1, no. 2 (2010), 263–76.
9   Raymond Lucas, *Sensory Notation Handbook*, self published, 2014, www.lulu.com/shop/raymond-lucas/sensory-notation-handbook-2014/paperback/product-21871919.html?ppn=1
10 Lawrence Hass, *Merleau-Ponty's Philosophy* (Bloomington and Indianapolis: Indiana University Press, 2008), 68–9.
11 Kent C. Bloomer and Charles W. Moore, *Body, Memory, and Architecture*, (New Haven: Yale University Press, 1977), 44.
12 Ibid., 92.
13 Steven Holl, "Questions of perception: phenomenology of architecture," in *Questions of Perception*, ed. Steven Holl, Juhani Pallasmaa, and Alberto Pérez-Gómez (San Francisco: William Stout Publishers), 41.
14 Linda Yablonsky, "Sound garden," *The New York Times, T Magazine*, April 1, 2012, M278.
15 Steve Erickson, "Doug Aitken is redefining how we experience art," *Smithsonian Magazine*, December 2013, www.smithsonianmag.com/innovation/doug-aitken-is-redefining-how-we-experience-art-180947643/#aylfI1VHjrg4i74j.99

16 Yablonsky, "Sound garden," M278.
17 Steve Erickson, "Doug Aitken is redefining how we experience art."
18 Steven Holl, *The Chapel of St. Ignatius* (New York: Princeton Architectural Press, 1999), 14.
19 Ibid., 16.
20 Ibid., 37.
21 "Faith 1996–1997," *Linda Beaumont*, www.lindabeaumont.com/index. php?page=publiccommissions&subcatID=8 (accessed July 20, 2016).
22 Pol Martin, "Vals Thermal Baths," *arcspace.com*, November 17, 2014, www. arcspace.com/features/atelier-peter-zumthor/vals-thermal-baths/
23 Ibid.
24 Ibid.
25 All temperatures are as listed in the Hotel Therme Vals Information and Prices Brochure, 2012/2013, www.therme-vals.ch/static/files/Informations_and_prices_englisch_2012_2013.pdf
26 Dean Hawkes, "The poetics of environment," in *Beyond Environmental Comfort*, ed. Bon Lay Ong (New York: Routledge, 2013), 134.
27 Michael Kimmelman, "The ascension of Peter Zumthor," *The New York Times Magazine*, March 11, 2011, www.nytimes.com/2011/03/13/magazine/mag-13zumthor-t.html?ref=michaelkimmelman&_r=0
28 Feda Vukic, "Natural mystic urban," in *Zadar: Sea Organ and Greeting to the Sun*, ed. Barbara Bašić Stelluti and Vladimir Mattioni (Zadar: Marinaprojekt d.o.o., 2011), 12.
29 Leo Modrcin, "Reflections," in *Zadar: Sea Organ and Greeting to the Sun*, ed. Barbara Bašić Stelluti and Vladimir Mattioni (Zadar: Marinaprojekt d.o.o., 2011), 60.
30 Vladimir Mattioni, "Foreword," in *Zadar: Sea Organ and Greeting to the Sun*, ed. Barbara Bašić Stelluti and Vladimir Mattioni (Zadar: Marinaprojekt d.o.o., 2011), 6.
31 Nikola Bašić, "Urban retorts," in *Zadar: Sea Organ and Greeting to the Sun*, ed. Barbara Bašić Stelluti and Vladimir Mattioni (Zadar: Marinaprojekt d.o.o., 2011), 27.
32 Ivan Stamać, "The sound component of Sea Organ," in *Zadar: Sea Organ and Greeting to the Sun*, ed. Barbara Bašić Stelluti and Vladimir Mattioni (Zadar: Marinaprojekt d.o.o., 2011), 41.
33 Zeljka Corak, "The place where the endless meets the definite," in *Zadar: Sea Organ and Greeting to the Sun*, ed. Barbara Bašić Stelluti and Vladimir Mattioni (Zadar: Marinaprojekt d.o.o., 2011), 50.
34 Modrcin, "Reflections," 103.

Time and Movement
Rituals of Change

Chapter 9

"When all the world appears to be in a tumult, and nature itself is feeling the assault of climate change, the seasons retain their essential rhythm. Yes, fall gives us a premonition of winter, but then, winter, will be forced to relent, once again, to the new beginnings of soft greens, longer light, and the sweet air of spring."[1]

Madeleine Kunin

"Warm bedroom, Barbara?" asked Radiya, our host, in her broken English each evening as darkness descended. It was both a thoughtful offer and her signal that the family was tired and ready for bed. I would nod and she would get up to light our bedroom fire. That was the only room in the house that was heated in winter besides the family room where we ate, talked and spent the rest of the day. The family also slept in this communal room, but as guests, my husband, daughter and I rated our own heated room at night. It was mid November in central Turkey. We were spending the month in a stone house perched at the edge of a ravine in a small Cappadocian village. The house was large, but it was customary to heat only one room in winter to save on fuel costs. So as snow fell outside and the stone walls radiated the cold inwards, we all huddled around the samovar stove in this one room. As I made my way from the warmth of this room to the bathroom or to the unheated kitchen to help with cooking, I sometimes wandered off to explore other rooms of the house, now closed and shuttered. I imagined how different the house must feel in summer when window covers were drawn back and sunlight poked into the dark corners. How spacious the house must feel, how full of light and life! But in November, the house curled in around one small room, hibernating, waiting for spring.

The natural rhythms of life from season to season and morning to night mark the progress of time as we inhabit a place. The sensescape evolves around us and we experience new smells, sounds, textures of light. They may change quickly with the brewing of a storm or slowly over the progression of seasons. The sensescape also evolves as we move our bodies from place to place. Again, the changes may be rapid as we move from inside to outside on a winter day or gradual as we walk from the city center to the countryside. In this chapter, we will explore this movement and change of sensory experience and how it adds a textural rhythm to our sensory world.

THE MOVING PLANET

In earlier chapters, we noted how the Earth's movement around the sun and around its own axis orchestrates a sensory rhythm to the cycle of a day or a year, narrating a story about the places we inhabit. These rhythms characterize each place and convey the passage of time. Pallasmaa reminds us that

> "We have a mental need to grasp that we are rooted in the continuity of time, and in the man-made world it is the task of architecture to facilitate this experience. Architecture domesticates limitless space and enables us to inhabit it, but it should likewise domesticate endless time and enable us to inhabit the continuum of time."[2]

In an insightful essay entitled "For those who spend time in a place,"[3] Ralph Knowles explores how the built environment can mark the passage of time like a sundial. He points out how the annual solar movement is especially noticeable in spaces (buildings, street grids and valleys) that are elongated from east to west (Figure 9.1). For these, the south-facing side is almost always in sun and the north-facing side in perpetual shadow; hence, the popularity of south-facing hillsides. If the east/west elongated space is a narrow street, as summer moves to winter, the shadows cast by the buildings lining the street's south side crawl northward across the street and up the opposite walls as the sun sinks lower in the sky. At winter solstice, the shadow line reverses its direction of travel, returning to its low point at the summer solstice. This complete cycle takes exactly one year.[4] The inhabitants of the adjacent houses live within either the wedge of sunlight or its interlocking

WINTER

SUMMER

Figure 9.1 In this east/west elongated street in Sweden, south-facing façades are bright with summer sunlight while a wedge of shadow clings to north façades. As winter approaches, the shadow line will move northward (right) across the street and up the south-facing façade, filling the street with shadow. At the solstice, it will reverse its direction of travel and move back down the wall, bringing sunlight again to the street.

wedge of shadow and, thus, have two very different experiences.

In contrast to this annual rhythm, daily solar rhythms are more rapid and flow from east to west. So this motion is most noticeable on streets or buildings that run north/ south. For these, the east-facing elevations are bathed in morning sunlight, which diminishes as the sun moves westward. At solar noon, the sunlight leaves the east-facing walls completely and west-facing elevations start to receive their daily share of light. Then, darkness descends and the cycle repeats. Inhabitants on either side of these north/

south streets mark time on a daily rhythm—morning sun and afternoon shade (or vice versa across the street).

Rhythms like these animate all of the sensory realms. In winter, acoustic and olfactory spaces in buildings shrink as windows are closed and shuttered. Thermal boundaries become more abrupt as colder outside temperatures exaggerate differences between inside and out. Color space evolves as sky conditions change, deciduous trees lose their leaves and blooming plants die back (Figure 9.2). Winds change direction and bring new odors, sounds and precipitation. These cycles trigger other sensory changes as they initiate annual or daily activities. Roosters crow; coffee is brewed; street vendors hawk their wares; grass is

Figure 9.2 This deck at the Barbouni Beach Restaurant in Costa Navarino, Greece (k-studio, 2013), is oriented to catch breezes off the sea. The gentle motion of fabric panels above the tables announces the arrival of the daily breeze, animating the sunlight and mimicking the wavy surface of the water.

Time and Movement: Rituals of Change

mowed; traffic snarls; onions and garlic are fried; and the call to prayer wafts out from the local mosque.

As we saw in Turkey, closing part of a building is one way to respond to seasonal changes. This is not just an outdated response to cold weather. A recent study for the National Park Service's net zero energy multi-agency building in Seward, Alaska, also took this approach. To save energy and tailor the building's size to the reduced number of visitors and staff during cold weather, its prospective design called for portions of the building to be totally or partially closed in winter. During summer months, on the other hand, the building was designed to open up to incorporate outdoor space into its exhibit and retail sales areas, thus expanding the building's operational size beyond its architectural boundaries. Although current plans for the building have changed, this initial study showed how the building's seasonal expansion and contraction could help achieve its net zero energy goal.

Migration, either within a geographic region or within a building, is another response to seasonal changes in the sensory environment. Historically, tribes of people migrated to follow seasonal food sources and to maintain thermal comfort. Now that we have more control over food and interior thermal conditions, our migrations are more pleasure oriented. Many of us migrate annually to the mountains in summer or to the tropics in winter.

But our travels don't have to take us so far from home. Migrations to more pleasant microclimates (pockets of warm or cool air, of light, of scent or of quiet, either within the landscape or in a building) are also common. In *Thermal Delight in Architecture*, Lisa Heschong describes daily migrations in a variety of cultures, noting that

"In Tunisia, for example, the traditional two-story house encloses a central courtyard with colonnades along all sides. In the summer when the sun is high, the colonnade creates a deep shade. The family spends the day in the interior rooms of the first floor where the thermal mass of the building best protects them from the sun's heat. At night they move out onto the open roof which quickly loses its heat to the clear night sky. In the wintertime the pattern is reversed."[5]

Similarly, Ralph Knowles relates how his family developed an annual rhythm of occupying their back porch:

"A neighbor's tree spreads over the south end of our porch. To catch the warm winter sun, we move our table northward. To sit in the cool summer shadow, we move our table southward. Back and forth, once each spring and again each fall, we carry the table across a shadow line."[6]

He celebrates the ritual that this seasonal rhythm adds to the life of his family and laments how "architecture, by depending too much on machines, has destroyed ritual as a mode of self-expression."[7]

THE MOVING BODY

As we move through a place, we enter a new relationship with it that often involves a variety of sensory experiences. Sometimes we are pulled toward a new sensory space by the desire for comfort. At other times, the sensescape just changes around us as we move through a place (Figure 9.3). We may experience the even rhythm of alternating sun and shade and the accompanying warm and cool feelings as we walk through the shadows of columns in a sunlit arcade or the less regular sequence of sounds and smells that envelop us from adjacent shops. Sensory rhythms speed up as we move faster. They may

Figure 9.3 In the direct sunlight, this arcade at the Great Mosque of Kairouan, Tunisia, creates a rhythm of sun and shadow spaces.

have a strobe-like effect if we're riding a bicycle or become a sensory blur if we drive by in a car.

There are many opportunities to feel rhythm in movement through sensory realms. The cadence and sound of stairs depends on the energy of the person descending. A landing interrupts the cadence. The tempo going up differs from that coming down. As we move through a rose garden, we may stop to smell a single flower from each bed, experiencing the intensity of smell, then resting with the less intense background odor before immersing ourselves again. Inhale, rest, inhale … weaving our way through the garden. It is often the rest, the space between, that intensifies the next inhale.

Sometimes when we are presented with a rhythmic structure at the right scale, we are enticed to explore its rhythm with another sensory realm. Coming upon a line of fence slats, we may be compelled to run our hand or a stick along them to feel the jagged rhythm with our body or hear the tap, tap, tap of sound. Or facing a crosswalk marked by a pattern of white lines perpendicular to our path, we may be drawn to hop from line to line or to step only on the spaces between them to create a rhythmic movement.

Movement into and through a building frequently generates a sensory entry sequence that builds to the final destination. The Broad Museum by Diller Scofidio + Renfro (2015) orchestrates the sensory experience to create a dramatic arrival at the main galleries on the third floor. The approach to the museum is unshaded, through the bright Los Angeles sunlight. As you move into the building from the intense exterior sunlight, you enter a lobby that *Architectural Record* describes as

> "dimly lit, gray—sculpted like massive rock formations. Though the facade forms a porous screen between streetscape and lobby, the space feels like a crypt or subterranean cavern. From the lobby, you board an extreme—105-foot-long—escalator that threads through a narrow sloped tunnel, resembling a shaft bored into boulders by the elements. Exciting yet incongruous, this straight shot up to the third-floor galleries recalls such improbable juxtapositions as the escalator in Perugia, Italy, rising to the city's upper precinct through archeological ruins, or the belief-suspending exhilaration of a theme-park ride. … And emerging from the darkened, tightly choreographed sequence—as you arrive beneath the daylit diagrid—is sublime."[8]

The job of a designer is to orchestrate the sequence of sensory experiences to increase the probability of delight. The designer may ask: Does the progression of sensory experience grow in intensity or lessen? Does it repeat in a rhythmic pattern? If so, is the rhythm intentional or a side effect of some other phenomenon? Is it a single "one note" in a field of silence, like the shaded tree in the grassland, or does it repeat in a random or rhythmical pattern? What is the score of these sensory rhythms?

CHOREOGRAPHING THE FLOW

A rhythm is a change in intensity or quality over time in a noticeable and meaningful pattern. The use of the word "meaningful" is important. It indicates a process that connects to a larger concept. The naturally occurring sensory rhythms that are caused by the Earth's movement are meaningful because they are predictable and integrally tied to place. In working with these rhythms, the designer anticipates their occurrence and provides places to celebrate them. Since many natural sensory experiences are related to place, taking advantage of their rhythms requires a thorough knowledge of the local climate and culture. A designer may work with these cyclic changes either to enhance a particular sensory aspect or to craft a contrasting sensory environment as an overlay. An enclosed building is in fact just that—a crafted sensory environment designed to provide thermal comfort and security in a sometimes uncomfortable or threatening exterior environment. But as we have seen, it doesn't require physical walls to create places of sensory intensity, and the sequencing of these sensory nodes is an important consideration in their design.

In creating the transition from one sensory experience to the next, a designer must first explore the underlying patterns of movement through the space and the cultural expectations along this path. At the Broad Museum, the usual path for most visitors is from the entryway to the main gallery on the third floor. The cultural expectation for this transition is a series of well-lit spaces that lead to the upper levels. In choosing to plunge the visitor into a darkened tunnel, the architect has created a tension in the entry sequence that makes the arrival at the gallery dramatic. Thus, done well, going against the cultural expectation has the possibility of increasing drama.

Designers should also consider the qualitative and quantitative differences between sensory spaces in a progression. Transitions may occur between spaces or times of varying sensory intensity (bright light to dim, loud noise to quiet, etc.) or different qualities (red space to green, salsa music to a slow waltz, etc.). The change between these conditions, either through space or through time, may be gradual or abrupt depending on the boundary gradient. For example, in the movement from outside to inside a building through a solid door, both the thermal space and the light space may change abruptly. This change may be a pleasant or an irritating shock to a body that has acclimated to the outside. On the other hand, moving from a hot, sunny field to the shade of a tree is a gradual change as one first encounters the dappled light at the edge of the leafy canopy and then enters the full shade of the tree.

As we move from one sensory experience to the next, the mixing of sensory inputs at the boundary is also important to consider. If the boundaries between two contrasting sensory spaces are gradual and overlap, the transition reflects a mix of the sensory experiences. For example, if two sound spaces overlap, the transition from one to the other moves through a blended sound space that can be quite distracting, as when the sound of rap music from a bedroom mixes with the sound of a television in the living room. If the boundaries are abrupt, on the other hand, the contrast between the two is exaggerated. Thus, the gradient of change from one sensory space to another (either through time or space) provides another dimension to design. When done poorly, it can mislead, confuse or overwhelm the occupant. But when done well, it can guide our movements and deepen our experience of place.

How we experience these transitions depends also on our speed of travel. Designers can adjust the transition by either shrinking or stretching the boundary experience or by speeding up/slowing down the rate of travel (Figure 9.4). An elevator rapidly moves visitors straight up from the first to the third floor, while a spiral staircase takes a more gradual and circuitous route. The designer should also consider the response time for the sensory systems involved. For example, depending on a person's age, the eye can take up to 30 minutes to fully adapt to a new light level. So in spaces that accommodate elderly people, the designer can create gradual transitions in light levels to allow occupants' eyes to adapt to changes between inside and outside or between dramatically different interior lighting environments such as encountered in darkened theaters.

The path of travel may be either direct or convoluted, constrained or open to the occupant's choice. When it is open, sensory sequences can encourage movement in a particular direction. We have seen how people are drawn toward light. We can also be drawn toward pleasant smells, comfortable temperatures and interesting sounds. Shoppers are enticed into stores by the smell of chocolate or coffee; tourists wander down alleys toward the sound of music; children dare each other to skip along a concrete path through a gushing urban fountain (Figure 9.5). And at each turn of the path, a new sensory world appears.

Figure 9.4 At Amar Children's Center (Dorte Mandrup Arkitekter, Copenhagen, 2013), children have the option of walking up the stairs or exploring the inclined climbing wall that engages their whole bodies as they ascend to the upper level.

Figure 9.5 The path through the fountain at Westlake Park in downtown Seattle moves dangerously close to the rushing water and envelopes visitors in thunderous sound.

Notes

1   Madeleine Kunin, "Seasons endings and beginnings," *The Huffington Post blog*, September 27, 2012, www.huffingtonpost.com/madeleine-m-kunin/madeleine-kunin-observes_b_1920500.html
2   Juhani Pallasmaa, *The Eyes of the Skin: Architecture and the Senses* (West Sussex: John Wiley & Sons, 2005), 32.
3   Ralph Knowles, "For those who spend time in a place," *Places* 8, no. 2 (1992), http://escholarship.org/uc/item/6v56t52x
4   Ibid.
5   Lisa Heschong, *Thermal Delight in Architecture* (Cambridge: The MIT Press, 1982), 8.
6   Knowles, "For those who spend time in a place."
7   Ibid.
8   Sarah Amelar, "Broad Museum," *Architectural Record*, September 16, 2015, http://archrecord.construction.com/projects/Building_Types_Study/museums/2015/1509-broad-museum-la.asp

A Sense of Place

Chapter 10

"As place is sensed, senses are placed; as places make sense, senses make place."[1]

Steven Feld

The choppy waves of Lake Washington slosh around our kayak as my husband excitedly points toward shore and says, "See that tree there? That's where my men's group meets." For the past ten years, I've been wondering where my husband and seven of his closest friends meet every Friday morning to talk about their lives and challenges just as the sun is rising. So I'm curious about this sacred spot in the woods, but I see nothing special—only a rocky beach lined with hundreds of potential trees. I probe for details. "The tall one with the branching trunk," he replies. I smile, knowing that he is seeing a cozy cleared area around the base of a single, special tree that I still can't identify from the score of others in the general direction he is pointing. I realize that he is feeling a particular log against his back and the chill of morning air. He's smelling the earthy dampness of rocky ground that slopes gently toward the water. He's squinting with the first sun's rays streaming through needled branches and hearing the cadence and tones of the voices of men he's shared this place with for the past decade, come rain or shine. It is not always "comfortable." This is Seattle, after all. When it rains, they huddle under tarps and umbrellas. But the years of meeting there have added an aura of communal familiarity to these shared feelings. For him, it is now a powerfully poignant place, clearly distinct from the forest surrounding it. Yet I still can't tell which tree he's pointing at.

We live in enchanted worlds filled with places invisible to others but brimming with shared experiences and memories for ourselves. We carry the knowing of these places in our bodies as much as in our minds. Our bodies relax into them or tense in fear depending on our past experiences there. Charged with memory, these places are noticeable to us, separate from their surroundings. We sense their boundaries, thresholds and centers even if they have no visible demarcations that can be noticed by others. So we may stroll past each other's special places ignorant of their existence, perhaps tripping over their sacred logs or drinking beer in their ceremonial alcoves.

These special places may be communal like my husband's sacred space in the woods, known only to a circle of friends. Or they may be personal like the brown velvet chair where I write. My body knows the soft nap of its fabric, the give of its foam lining against my back, the warmth from the heating duct above it, its cozy darkness contrasted with the bright window corner across the room. It carries memories just as it holds the coffee stain I made when I jumped up too quickly to answer the door. Whether they are communal or private, we cherish these places charged with meaning, sometimes jealously claiming them. We smile when we see a friend awaiting us at our regular Tuesday morning coffeehouse table, but our heart sinks in disappointment at finding someone else in *our* library carrel or on *our* park bench. In fact, we are peeved at them for trespassing on *our* territory (Figure 10.1). How childish and yet how common these feelings of ownership are. How dear is this connection to place!

ATMOSPHERE

What is it that changes *space* into memorable *place*? We call this quality of place its ambiance or atmosphere. Runkel and Wesener describe these ethereal qualities as

"noticeable but transitory environmental qualities, not directly attached to physical entities but inexistent without [them], possessing the ability to capture people's sensuous conditions in particular situations. ... Atmospheres are mediations between subject and the reality of the sensed world. They are not directly

Figure 10.1 We cherish and claim our special places in the world and these territories live on in our collective memories. Sculptor Fernando Mayoral honored the memory of writer Gonzalo Torrente Ballester with a sculpture of him seated in his favorite writing spot at Café Novelty in Salamanca, Spain. Even after his death, Ballester continues to claim this special corner.

perceived, but rather influence the conditions under which phenomena emerge and appear to the senses. They are felt by the body rather than cognitively understood."[2]

They are essences of place—what Pallasmaa calls a lived metaphor[3] and what Runkel and Wesener call the "place-bound construction of individual and collective memories."[4] They have been the object of study throughout the history of design, but their elusive nature makes them difficult to describe. In *Genius Loci*, Christian Norberg-Schultz emphasizes how

The cultural importance of defining an area which is qualitatively different from the surroundings, cannot be overestimated. The *temenos* is the archetypal form of meaningful space, and constitutes the point of departure for human settlement. ... When several fields interact, a complex spatial structure results, of varying density, tension and dynamism."[5] (See Figure 10.2.)

In recent years, a resurgence of interest in understanding this dynamic tension of place encouraged the formation of an International Ambiances Network[6] with the goal of promoting the sensory domain in the questioning and design of lived space. This network and its associated international conferences bring together a multidisciplinary group of professionals in the fields of architecture and urban planning, human and social sciences, engineering and applied physics, and the arts. Their work clearly points to the senses as pivotal links that connect the exterior world with our inner experience of place. One of the understandings that emerges from this work is the iterative communication between person and place that is mediated through the senses.

TERRITORY

One aspect of this interaction is the way in which a *place* is shaped by the number of people who occupy it and, in turn, defines and limits the size of the social group it accommodates. Sensory boundaries help to shape interactions among people. The extent of radiation of heat around a campfire circumscribes a bounded area of warmth, effectively limiting the number of people who can comfortably gather around it. The angle and distance of theater stage lighting defines how many actors can share the spotlight. The size of congregations in Reformation churches both determined and was determined by the acoustical characteristics of the building and music/vocalizations within it.

A Sense of Place

Figure 10.2 Cutting away stone in this underground cave at Windows of the Earth Cave Sanctuary (New Mexico), Ra Paulette has transformed space into sensuous place—an ethereal atmosphere that calls for hands to touch and explore its surfaces in their sinuous journey toward the light.

Buildings are assigned maximum occupancies, but the boundaries of sensory space frequently prescribe a smaller number and/or distribute occupants unevenly within the defined geometry of the building or room. In *A Pattern Language*, Christopher Alexander and his co-writers acknowledge this effect:

> "It is a fact of human nature that the space we use as social space is in part defined by light. When the light is perfectly even, the social function of the space gets utterly destroyed: it even becomes difficult for people to form natural human groups. If a group is in an area of uniform illumination, there are no light gradients corresponding to the boundary of the group, so the definition, cohesiveness and 'existence' of the group will be weakened. If the group is within a 'pool' of light, whose size and boundaries correspond to those of the group, this enhances the definition, cohesiveness, and even the phenomenological existence of the group."[7]

MEMORY/RITUAL/CULTURE

Another aspect of this complementary relationship is how the sense of place both creates new memories and evokes past place-bound memories. As we encounter a place with a certain ambiance, we are both drawn to that ambiance and reminded of times we have encountered it before, reliving all of the private and cultural connotations of those prior experiences. We build these body memories as individuals, groups or entire cultures. We may think of these personal/cultural space memories as "fragrances" that previous inhabitants left behind. As we pass through these places, we are aware of the past presence of the gathering (Figure 10.3). We identify with these places; they speak to us of belonging. We choose them because of the inclinations of our cultural heritage and they, in

Figure 10.3 A sliver of sunlight calls out the active café tables on this narrow pedestrian walkway in Athens. The sunspace defines which side of the walkway opens to the tables; the width determines how many can be accommodated. Repeated gatherings here build up collective understandings of connection and belonging.

turn, continue to shape our culture. Their use over time strengthens our connection with them and with our collective cultural memory.

As Lisa Heschong notes,

"The association of comfort with people and place [is] reinforced by the ritualized use of a place. Using a place at a set time and in a specific manner, as the Japanese use their baths, creates a constancy as dependable as the place itself. It establishes, in time and behavior, a definition of the place as strong as any architectural spatial definition. ... Through ritual, a place becomes an essential element in the customs of a people."[8]

The cultural nature of these experiences is significant. Our cultures define which ambiances we are drawn to and we are, in turn, shaped by those same ambiances. So the experience of ambiance may not translate well between cultures. A late-night gathering of men around a charcoal fire in a metal drum may appear menacing to a visitor in unfamiliar territory but is experienced as a cozy social node to cultural insiders. As Hall points out in *The Hidden Dimension*,

"Space perception is not only a matter of what can be perceived but what can be screened out. People brought up in different cultures learn as children, without ever knowing that they have done so, to screen out one type of information while paying close attention to another. ... The Japanese, for example, screen visually in a variety of ways but are perfectly content with paper walls as acoustic screens. Spending the night at a Japanese inn while a party is going on next door is a new sensory experience for the Westerner. In contrast, the Germans and the Dutch depend on thick walls and double doors to screen sound, and have difficulty if they must rely on their own powers of concentration to screen out sound. If two rooms are the same size and one screens out sound but the other one doesn't, the sensitive German who is trying to concentrate will feel less crowded in the former because he feels less intruded on."[9]

A Sense of Place

GEOGRAPHY

Earlier, we noted how geographic location determines the sun's height and path through the sky. This dependable solar trajectory endows the cardinal orientations with attributes of light and heat with different daily and annual rhythms, creating pockets of heat and light both inside and outside. We have seen how we migrate from sunlight to shadow depending on the climate and our desire for warmth or coolness. We also noted how clouds and rainfall change the quality of light and sound and smells, and how our bodies register the rise or flatness of the ground that stretches before us. We have felt the texture of the local rock, the smell of regional plants in bloom. We have explored how these natural elements hold within them the subtle touch of history and memory that synthetic materials don't have.

These peculiarities of the local environment sculpt our cultural affinities for the places we inhabit and our bodies change to accommodate their sensory personalities. We are both drawn to the ambiance of a place and are shaped by it. It is a symbiosis that is mediated by the senses. In Chapter 3, I related how the oyster light of the Pacific Northwest both drew me to Seattle and, over the years, reinforced this place as my home. I have "grown my gills" as the locals sometimes say. Each of us partners in this dance with place as we settle into our particular niche of the world. Or as Christian Norberg-Schultz points out in *Genius Loci*, this identification "means that we become 'friends' with a particular environment."[10]

SENSE AND SUSTAINABILITY

In short, our senses ground us in place and our place grounds us in the world. As Lawrence Hass notes, this deep connection speaks to the critical importance of a return to the senses. This new undertaking that Hass calls the "virtue of sensibility" has the potential to

> "save us from environmental disaster by illuminating the natural world and exposing the abstractions that have supported its mindless appropriation and abuse. Less globally, this virtue is also about our health and wellbeing, about thinking in consonance with what we live, rather than in contradiction to it."[11]

The attention to sensory design is not separate from but, in many ways, arises with the desire for a sustainable, thriving existence on Earth. Many pragmatic approaches to design focusing on passive energy and energy efficiency create sensory texture, not merely as a byproduct but as a generative principle. Passive designs work with natural flows of light and heat to create comfortable and dynamic sensory environments. The glow of direct sunlight may call out significant nodes and gathering spaces; the shadowed corner may provide a cool refuge. Local materials create regional patterns of texture and rhythms of form. Even engineered systems find efficiency through the careful shaping of sensory space. Rather than conditioning an entire space, sustainable designs often provide a "tent" of task lighting under which more demanding tasks can be performed or an alcove of warmth or coolness where people can gather to be refreshed.

But below these pragmatics is an underpinning of connection to place that may be sensory design's strongest contribution to a sustainable future. The relationship between place and culture allows us to know and love ourselves and our community. Without that, we search for meaning elsewhere and cling to what the media tells us is fashionable. This love of place is critical for our planet, which is tipping the delicate balance of sustainability, because as Baba Dioum reminds us, "in the end we will conserve only what we love."[12]

SENSING THE FUTURE

A sense of place arises from the intricate interaction between place and people. It does not reside in either one but, rather, emerges from the life that occurs within it. As designers, we cannot guarantee this sense of place. We can neither predetermine what its occupants will attend to, nor design their shared memories. But by paying attention to our body's delight at nodes of sensory intensity or whimsical illusions and attending to the flow of time and movement, we can design places of sensory richness that encourage people to linger and memories to cling.

Creating such spaces requires us to be awake to our bodies and their sensory delights. It requires also cross-disciplinary design teams working together toward a common vision. This vital work can no longer tolerate a handoff of responsibility from the designer to the engineer to the occupant but, rather, requires an integrated team of collaborators who share a common language and understanding of the sensory world. The resulting multisensory designs may consist of overlapping sensory volumes that intensify the use of a cultural space or they may contrast individual sensory space experiences to create mystery and playful illusions. They may provide a variety of spaces or experiences that allow occupants to move into their preference of warmth, light, sound or quiet.

Ultimately, this work is about reconnecting with the world around us. Neither abstracted to the perfect distant perspective nor flattened to a generic beige, our built environment will entice us with its brilliant shades of vermillion and chartreuse, its steamy baths, chilly shadows, hushed silences, thundering echoes, sunny window seats, aromatic plants and polished banisters. We will touch and smell and hear and dance with the world in all its sensory richness. Drawn to the special atmosphere of place, alone or with a community of friends, we will celebrate the sensuous world surrounding us and know it as home.

Notes

1   Steven Feld, "Waterfalls of song: an acoustemology of place resounding in Bosavi, Papua New Guinea," chapter 3 in *Senses of Place*, ed. Steven Feld and Keith H. Basso (Santa Fe: School of American Research Press, 1996), 91.
2   Simon Runkel and Andreas Wesener, "'Rencontre sur les Lieux': Memory Construction in Urban Ambiances," in *Ambiances in Action, Proceedings of the 2nd International Congress on Ambiances*, ed. Jean-Paul Thibaud and Daniel Siret (Ambianced International Network, 2012), 121–2.
3   Juhani Pallasmaa, *The Embodied Image: Imagination and Imagery in Architecture* (West Sussex: John Wiley & Sons, 2011), 67.
4   Runkel and Wesener, "'Rencontre sur les Lieux,'" 121.
5   Christian Norberg-Schulz, *Genius Loci: Towards a Phenomenology of Architecture* (New York: Rizzoli, 1980), 58, 61.
6   International Ambiances Network, www.ambiances.net/home.html
7   Christopher Alexander, Sara Ishikawa, and Murray Silverstein, with Max Jacobson, Ingrid Fiksdahl-King and Shlomo Angel, *A Pattern Language: Towns-Buildings-Construction* (New York: Oxford University Press, 1977), 1161.
8   Lisa Heschong, *Thermal Delight in Architecture* (Cambridge: The MIT Press, 1982), 49.
9   Edward T. Hall, *The Hidden Dimension* (New York: Anchor Books, 1990), 45.
10 Norberg-Shulz, *Genius Loci*, 21.
11 Lawrence Hass, *Merleau-Ponty's Philosophy* (Bloomington and Indianapolis: Indiana University Press, 2008), 71.
12 Baba Dioum as quoted by JoAnn M. Valenti and Gaugau Tavana, "Report: continuing science education for environmental journalists and science writers (in situ with the experts)," *Science Communication* 27, no. 2 (2005), 308.

Selected Bibliography

"Blind as a bat: seeing without eyesight." *YouTube*, July 18, 2011 [video]. https://www.youtube.com/watch?v=Z_E3zxx2l9g.

"Immersed, sound and architecture." *OASE* 78 (2009). www.oasejournal.nl/en/Issues/78 (accessed July 20, 2016).

"Resonant form: the convergence of sound and space." *Shea Trahan*. www.sheatrahan.com/#!project-1/c1o27 (accessed July 20, 2016).

Abram, David. *Becoming Animal: An Earthly Cosmology*. New York: Vintage Books, 2010.

Ackerman, Diane. *A Natural History of the Senses*. London: Phoenix, a division of Orion Books Ltd., 2000.

Alexander, Christopher, Sara Ishikawa, and Murray Silverstein, with Max Jacobson, Ingrid Fiksdahl-King and Shlomo Angel. *A Pattern Language: Towns-Buildings-Construction*. New York: Oxford University Press, 1977.

Amelar, Sarah. "Broad Museum." *Architectural Record*, September 16, 2015. http://archrecord.construction.com/projects/Building_Types_Study/museums/2015/1509-broad-museum-la.asp

Anderson, Mark. "Do vibrations help us smell?" *Scientific American*, April 1, 2013. www.scientificamerican.com/article/do-vibrations-help-us-smell/

Angry Architect, The. "The architecture of perception: 5 spaces designed to stimulate your senses." *Architizer*, February 25, 2015. http://architizer.com/blog/the-architecture-of-perception/

Bachelard, Gaston. *The Poetics of Space*. Translated by Maria Jolas. Boston: Beacon Press, 1969.

Bainbridge, David, and Ken Haggard. *Passive Solar Architecture: Heating, Cooling, Ventilation, Daylighting and More Using Natural Flows*. Vermont: Chelsea Green Publishing, 2011.

Banham, Reyner. *The Architecture of the Well-tempered Environment*. Chicago: The University of Chicago Press, 1969.

Banissy, Michael J., and Jamie Ward. "Mirror-touch synesthesia is linked with empathy." *Nature Neuroscience*, June 17, 2007. www.daysyn.com/Banissy_Wardpublished.pdf

Barbara, Anna, and Anthony Perliss. *Invisible Architecture: Experiencing Places through the Sense of Smell*. Milano: SKIRA Press, 2006.

Bašić Stelluti, Barbara, and Vladimir Mattioni (eds.). *Zadar: Sea Organ and Greeting to the Sun*. Zadar: Marinaprojekt d.o.o., 2011.

Beaumont, Linda. "Faith 1996–1997," *Linda Beaumont*. www.lindabeaumont. com/index.php?page=publiccommissions&subcatID=8 (accessed July 20, 2016).

Belluck, Pam. "Chilly at work? Office formula was designed for men." *The New York Times*, August 3, 2015. www.nytimes.com/2015/08/04/science/chilly-at-work-a-decades-old-formula-may-be-to-blame.html

Benedikt, Michael. "Environmental stoicism and place machismo." *Harvard Design Magazine* (Winter/Spring, 2002), 1–8.

Bensmaia, Sliman J., and Jeffrey M. Yau. "The organization and function of somatosensory cortex." In *The Handbook of Touch: Neuroscience, Behavioral, and Health Perspectives*, edited by Matthew J. Hertenstein and Sandra J. Weiss. New York: Springer Publishing Company, 2011, pp. 161–88.

Bies, David A., and Colin H. Hansen. *Engineering Noise Control: Theory and Practice*, 4th Edition. London: Spon Press, 2009.

Blesser, Barry, and Linda-Ruth Salter. *Spaces Speak, Are You Listening?* Cambridge: The MIT Press, 2009.

Bloomer, Kent C., and Charles W. Moore. *Body, Memory, and Architecture*. New Haven: Yale University Press, 1977.

Bushdid, C., M. O. Magnasco, L. B. Vosshall, and A. Keller. "Humans can discriminate more than one trillion olfactory stimuli." *Science*, March 21, 2014, 1370–2.

Byrne, David. "How architecture helped music evolve." *TED* [video], 2010, https://www.ted.com/talks/david_byrne_how_architecture_helped_music_evolve?language=en#t-593858.

Cavanaugh, William J., and Gregory C. Tocci. *Architectural Acoustics: Principles and Practice*. New Jersey: John Wiley & Sons, 2010.

Chebat, Jean-Charles, and Richard Michon. "Impact of ambient odours on mall shoppers' emotions, cognition, and spending: a test of competitive causal theories." *Journal of Business Research* 56, no. 7 (July 2003), 529–39.

Cytowic, Richard E. *The Man Who Tasted Shapes*. Cambridge: The MIT Press, 2003.

Day, Christopher. *Places of the Soul*, 2nd Edition. Oxford: Elsevier Ltd., 2008.

De Dear, Richard, and Gail Schiller Brager. "Developing an adaptive model of thermal comfort and preference." *ASHRAE Transactions* 104, no.1 (1998), 145–67.

DeKay, Mark, and G. Z. Brown. *Sun, Wind, and Light: Architectural Design Strategies*, 3rd Edition. New Jersey: John Wiley & Sons, 2014.

Egan, Timothy. "Tacoma journal; on good days, the smell can hardly be noticed." *The New York Times*, April 3, 1988. www.nytimes.com/1988/04/06/us/tacoma-journal-on-good-days-the-smell-can-hardly-be-noticed.html

Erickson, Steve. "Doug Aitken is redefining how we experience art." *Smithsonian Magazine*, December 2013. www.smithsonianmag.

com/innovation/doug-aitken-is-redefining-how-we-experience-art-180947643/#aylfI1VHjrg4i74j.99 (accessed July 20, 2016).

Ermann, Michael. *Architectural Acoustics Illustrated*. Hoboken: John Wiley & Sons, 2015.

Fehrman, Kenneth R., and Cherie Fehrman. *Color: The Secret Influence*. New Jersey: Prentice-Hall Inc., 2000.

Feld, Steven, and Keith H. Basso (eds.). *Senses of Place*. Santa Fe: School of American Research Press, 1996.

Foy, George Michelson. "Experience: I've been to the quietest place on Earth." *The Guardian*, May 18, 2012. www.theguardian.com/lifeandstyle/2012/may/18/experience-quietest-place-on-earth

Goldstein, E. Bruce. *Sensation and Perception*, 8th Edition. Belmont: Wadsworth, Cengage Learning, 2007.

Goller, Bea. "Sound as space generator." *Architecture and Sound Research*. https://sonomorphism.wordpress.com/writings/sound-as-space-generator/ (accessed July 20, 2016).

Gordinier, Jeff. "Restaurants take the din out of dining." *The New York Times*, September 4, 2015.

Gordon, Gary. *Interior Lighting for Designers*. Hoboken: John Wiley & Sons, 2003.

Gudrais, Elizabeth. "The power of touch." *Harvard Magazine*, November–December, 2010. http://harvardmagazine.com/2010/11/the-power-of-touch (accessed July 20, 2016).

Hall, Edward T. *The Hidden Dimension*. New York: Anchor Books, 1990.

Harlow, Harry F. "The nature of love." *American Psychologist* 13 (December 1958), 673–85.

Hass, Lawrence. *Merleau-Ponty's Philosophy*. Bloomington and Indianapolis: Indiana University Press, 2008.

Henry, Christopher N. "Tactile architecture: does it matter?" *ArchDaily*, November 23, 2011. www.archdaily.com/186499/tactile-architecture-does-it-matter.

Henshaw, Victoria. *Urban Smellscapes: Understanding and Designing City Smell Environments*. New York: Routledge, 2014.

Henshaw, Victoria. "Scents of place: the power of the olfactory." *The Architectural Review*, August 3, 2014. www.architectural-review.com/archive/scents-of-place-the-power-of-the-olfactory/8666675.fullarticle

Henshaw, Victoria. "Fragrant cities, relationships between smell and environments." cities@manchester blog. https://citiesmcr.wordpress.com/2012/03/05/fragrant-cities-relationships-between-smell-and-urban-environments/ (accessed July 20, 2016).

Herssens, Jasmien, Ann Heylighen, and K. U. Leuven. "Haptic design research: a blind sense of place." *Proceedings of the ARCC/EAAE 2010 International Conference on Architectural Research*, Washington, DC, June 23–26, 2010. www.aia.org/aiaucmp/groups/aia/documents/pdf/aiab087187.pdf

Herz, Rachel. *The Scent of Desire: Discovering Our Enigmatic Sense of Smell*. New York: Harper Collins Publishers, 2007.

Heschong, Lisa. *Thermal Delight in Architecture*. Cambridge: The MIT Press, 1982.

Holl, Steven. *The Chapel of St. Ignatius*. New York: Princeton Architectural Press, 1999.

Holl, Steven. "The Pantheon: A lesson on designing with light." Studio 360 [video], April 2, 2015. www.studio360.org/story/aha-moment-steven-holl-at-the-pantheon/

Holl, Steven, Juhani Pallasmaa, and Alberto Pérez-Gómez (eds.). *Questions of Perception*. San Francisco: William Stout Publishers, 2006.

Hosey, Lance. *The Shape of Green: Aesthetics, Ecology, and Design*. Washington: Island Press, 2012.

Hosey, Lance. "Scent and the city." *The New York Times*, Sunday Review, October 25, 2013.

Howes, David (ed.). *Empire of the Senses: The Sensual Culture Reader*. Oxford: Berg, 2006.

Hume, Lynne. *Portals: Opening Doorways to Other Realities through the Senses*. Oxford: Berg, 2007.

International Ambiances Network project. www.ambiances.net/home.html (accessed July 20, 2016).

Jarrett, Christian. *Great Myths of the Brain*. West Sussex: John Wiley & Sons, 2015.

Johnstone, Stephen, and Graham Ellard. "Anthony McCall by Stephen Johnstone & Graham Ellard." *BOMB* 97, Fall 2006. http://bombmagazine.org/article/2841/anthony-mccall (accessed July 20, 2016).

Kelly, Richard. "Lighting as an integral part of architecture." *College of Art Journal* 12, no. 1 (Autumn 1952), 24–30.

Kimmelman, Michael. "The ascension of Peter Zumthor." *The New York Times Magazine*, March 11, 2011. www.nytimes.com/2011/03/13/magazine/mag-13zumthor-t.html?ref=michaelkimmelman&_r=0

Kimmelman, Michael. "Dear architects: sound matters." *The New York Times*, Critic's Notebook, December 29, 2015. www.nytimes.com/interactive/2015/12/29/arts/design/sound-architecture.html?hp&action=click&pgtype=Homepage&clickSource=story-heading&module=photo-spot-region&region=top-news&WT.nav=top-news

Knowles, Ralph. "For those who spend time in a place." *Places* 8, no. 2 (1992). http://escholarship.org/uc/item/6v56t52x

Knowles, Ralph L. "The solar envelope." Personal web page, 1999. www-bcf.usc.edu/~rknowles/sol_env/sol_env.html (accessed July 20, 2016).

Koerth-Baker, Maggie. "What does it mean to be comfortable?" *The New York Times Magazine*, January 25, 2013. www.nytimes.com/2013/01/27/magazine/what-does-it-mean-to-be-comfortable.html

Kortrijk. "Arcades by Troika." *Disegno*, October 29, 2012. www.disegnodaily.com/article/arcades-by-troika

Lally, Sean. *The Air from Other Planets: A Brief History of Architecture to Come*. Zurich: Lars Müller Publishers, 2013.

Linden, David. *Touch, The Science of Heart, Hand and Mind*. New York: Viking, the Penguin Group, 2015.

Lindh, Ulrika Wänström. *Light Shapes Spaces: Experiences of Distribution of Light and Visual Spatial Boundaries*. PhD dissertation, HDK—School of Design and Crafts, University of Gothenburg, Sweden, 2012.

Long, Marshall. *Architectural Acoustics*, 2nd Edition. Oxford: Academic Press, 2014.

Low, Kelvin E. Y. *Scents and Scent-Sibilities: Smell and Everyday Life Experiences*. Newcastle Upon Tyne: Cambridge Scholars Publishing, 2009.

Lucas, Raymond. *Sensory Notation Handbook*. Self published, 2014. www.lulu. com/shop/raymond-lucas/sensory-notation-handbook-2014/paperback/ product-21871919.html?ppn=1

Lucas, Raymond, and Ombretta Romice. "Assessing the multi-sensory qualities of urban space: a methodological approach and notational system for recording and designing the multi-sensory experience of urban space." *Psychology* 1, no.2 (2010), 263–76.

Mace, Valerie. "Sensing the urban interior." Plenary Session: [in]arch International Conference, Java, Indonesia, September 10–11, 2014. https:// www.academia.edu/8379344/Sensing_the_Urban_Interior

Mahnke, Frank H. "Color in architecture, more than just decoration." *Archinect Features*, July 20, 2012. http://archinect.com/features/article/53292622/ color-in-architecture-more-than-just-decoration

Malnar, Joy Monice, and Frank Vodvarka. *Sensory Design*. Minneapolis: University of Minnesota Press, 2004.

Martin, Pol. "Vals Thermal Baths." *arcspace.com*. November 17, 2014. www. arcspace.com/features/atelier-peter-zumthor/vals-thermal-baths/

Meyers, Victoria. *Invisible Buildings*. www.victoriameyers.com/page/2/ (accessed November 17, 2015).

Michel, Lou. *Light: The Shape of Space*. New York: Van Nostrand Reinhold, 1996.

Millet, Marietta S. *Light Revealing Architecture*. New York: Van Nostrand Reinhold, 1996.

Moody, Fred. "In praise of Seattle light." *The Weekly: Seattle's Newsmagazine*, January 21–27, 1987, 28–32.

Norberg-Schulz, Christian. *Genius Loci: Towards a Phenomenology of Architecture*. New York: Rizzoli, 1980.

Ong, Boon Lay. "Warming up to heat." *Senses & Society* 7, issue 1 (2012), 5–21.

Ong, Boon Lay (ed.). *Beyond Environmental Comfort*. New York: Routledge, 2013.

Osman, Ashraf. *Overview of Olfactory Art in the 20th Century*. CAS Seminar Paper, June 24, 2013. https://www.academia.edu/4608919/Historical_ Overview_of_Olfactory_Art_in_the_20th_Century_CAS_Seminar_ Paper_

Otero-Pailos, Jorge. "An olfactory reconstruction of Philip Johnson's Glass House interior." In *After Taste: Expanded Practice in Interior Design*, edited by Kent Kleinman, Joanna Merwood-Salisbury, and Lois Weinthal. New York: Princeton Architectural Press, 2012, pp. 193–211.

Palipane, K. "Towards a sensory production of urban space: developing a conceptual framework of inquiry based on socio-sensory perception." Paper presented at the International RC21 Conference, *The struggle to Belong: Dealing with Diversity in 21st Century Urban Settings*, Amsterdam, 7–9 July, 2011.

Pallasmaa, Juhani. *The Eyes of the Skin: Architecture and the Senses*. West Sussex: John Wiley & Sons, 2005.

Pallasmaa, Juhani. *The Embodied Image: Imagination and Imagery in Architecture*. West Sussex: John Wiley & Sons, 2011.

Palmer, Alun. "20 fascinating facts about our sense of smell." *Mirror*, June 22, 2013, www.mirror.co.uk/lifestyle/health/20-fascinating-facts-sense-smell-1977351

Parkinson, Thomas, and Richard de Dear. "Thermal pleasure in built environments: physiology of alliesthesia." *Building Research and Information* 43, no. 3 (2015), 288–301.

Parsons, Chris. "Could Cockneys soon be brown bread?" *Daily Mail*, June 26, 2012. www.dailymail.co.uk/news/article-2164799/Bow-Bells-mark-area-true-Londoners-drowned-capitals-noise-pollution.html#ixzz3qvu35k00

Patel, Raj. "The Arup SoundLab," *Arup*. www.arup.com/Services/Acoustic_Consulting/SoundLab_Overview.aspx (accessed July 20, 2016).

Phillips, Derek. *Daylighting: Natural Light in Architecture*. Oxford: Architectural Press, 2004.

Pijanowski, Bryan. Record the Earth project. Purdue University. https://www.recordtheearth.org/ (accessed July 20, 2016).

Rasmussen, Steen Eiler. *Experiencing Architecture*. Cambridge: The MIT Press, 1982.

Redd, W. H., S. L. Manne, B. Peters, P. B. Jacobsen, and H. Schmidt. "Fragrance administration to reduce patient anxiety in MRI." *Journal of Magnetic Resonance Imaging* 4, no. 4 (1994), 623–6.

Robinson, Sarah, and Juhani Pallasmaa (eds.). *Mind in Architecture: Neuroscience, Embodiment and the Future of Design*. Cambridge: The MIT Press, 2015.

Roth, Leland M., and Amanda C. Roth Clark. *Understanding Architecture: Its Elements, History, and Meaning*. Boulder: Westview Press, 2014.

Runkel, Simon, and Andreas Wesener. "'Rencontre sur les lieux': memory construction in urban ambiances." In *Ambiances in Action, Proceedings of the 2nd International Congress on Ambiances*, edited by Jean-Paul Thibaud and Daniel Siret. Ambiances International Network, 2012, pp. 121–2.

Schafer, R. Murray. *The Soundscape: Our Sonic Environment and the Tuning of the World*. Rochester: Destiny Books, 1994.

Schuler, Timothy A. "The evolution of white light." *Architectural Lighting*, August 12, 2015. www.archlighting.com/technology/the-evolution-of-white-light_o

Sennett, Richard. *Flesh and Stone: The Body and the City in Western Civilization*. New York: W. W. Norton & Company, 1996.

Sound Tourism. *A Sonic Guide to Sonic Wonders*. www.sonicwonders.org/ (accessed July 20, 2016).

Swirnoff, Lois. *Dimensional Color*. Boston: Birkhauser, 1988.

Synnott, Anthony. *The Body Social: Symbolism, Self and Society*. London: Routledge, 1993.

Tanizaki, Jun'ichiro. *In Praise of Shadows*. Stony Creek: Leete's Island Books, 1997.

Taylor, Kate. "The smells of summer." *The New York Times*, August 19, 2015. www.nytimes.com/interactive/2015/08/20/nyregion/new-york-city-summer-smells.html

Thibaud, Jean-Paul, and Daniel Siret. *Ambiances in Action: Proceedings of the 2nd International Congress on Ambiances*. International Ambiances Network, 2012.

Thompson, Emily. *The Soundscape of Modernity: Architectural Acoustics and the Culture of Listening in America, 1900–1933*. Cambridge: The MIT Press, 2004.

Tobin, Desmond John. "The anatomy and physiology of the skin." In *The Handbook of Touch: Neuroscience, Behavioral, and Health Perspectives*, edited by Matthew J. Hertenstein and Sandra J. Weiss. New York: Springer Publishing Company, 2011, pp. 3–32.

Torcellini, P., N. Long, S. Pless, and R. Judkoff. *Evaluation of the Low-Energy Design and Energy Performance of the Zion National Park Visitors Center*. NREL/TP-550-34607. Colorado: National Renewable Energy Laboratory, February 2005.

Torrence, Jim, and Don Lemon with "Diamond Jim" and the Jazzmasters. *The Aroma of Tacoma*, Panjo Records, February 14, 2015 [video]. www.youtube.com/watch?v=uw_3aC-avjc

Trahan, Shea. "TED talk: the architecture of sound." *YouTube*, October 13, 2015 [video]. https://www.youtube.com/watch?v=R-BMF4e-1bg

Tuan, Yi-Fu. *Space and Place: The Perspective of Experience*. Minneapolis: University of Minnesota Press, 2008.

University of Salford. Sound Around You project. www.soundaroundyou.com/# (accessed July 20, 2016).

Watson, Donald, and Kenneth Labs. *Climatic Building Design: Energy-Efficient Building Principles and Practices*. New York City: McGraw-Hill, 1993.

Yablonsky, Linda. "Sound garden." *The New York Times*, T Magazine, April 1, 2012, M278.

Zumthor, Peter. *Atmospheres*. Basel: Birkhauser, 2006.

Zumthor, Peter. *Thinking Architecture*, 3rd Edition. Basel: Birkhauser, 2010.

Index

Page numbers in *italics* indicate illustrations, n indicates an endnote.